Your
Horoscope
2023

. . . .

Scorpio

24 October – 22 November

igloobooks

igloobooks

Published in 2022
First published in the UK by Igloo Books Ltd
An imprint of Igloo Books Ltd
Cottage Farm, NN6 0BJ, UK
Owned by Bonnier Books
Sveavägen 56, Stockholm, Sweden
www.igloobooks.com

0722 001
2 4 6 8 10 9 7 5 3 1
ISBN 978-1-80108-406-2

Written by Sally Kirkman
Additional content by Belinda Campbell and Denise Evans

Designed by Richard Sykes
Edited by Suzanne Fossey

Printed and manufactured in China

CONTENTS

. . . .

INTRODUCTION
. . . .

This 15-month guide has been designed and written to give a concise and accessible insight into both the nature of your star sign and the year ahead. Divided into two main sections, the first section of this guide will give you an overview of your character in order to help you understand how you think, perceive the world and interact with others and – perhaps just as importantly – why. You'll soon see that your zodiac sign is not just affected by a few stars in the sky, but by planets, elements, and a whole host of other factors, too.

The second section of this guide is made up of daily forecasts. Use these to increase your awareness of what might appear on your horizon so that you're better equipped to deal with the days ahead. While this should never be used to dictate your life, it can be useful to see how your energies might be affected or influenced, which in turn can help you prepare for what life might throw your way.

By the end of these 15 months, these two sections should have given you a deeper understanding and awareness of yourself and, in turn, the world around you. There are never any definite certainties, but with an open mind you will find guidance for what might be, and learn to take more control of your own destiny.

THE CHARACTER OF THE SCORPION

· · · · · · · · · · · · · · · · ·

Highly intimate, transformative, and controlled, Scorpios are the seducers of the zodiac calendar that are hard to resist. Whilst the affection of a Scorpio can be addictive, their passion can quickly feel possessive, so don't enter a serious relationship with this intense sign lightly. If you get on the wrong side of this powerful sign, whether it's by hurting them or someone that they fiercely love, then prepare yourself for an almighty sting from this Scorpion's tail. Just as their love is unforgettable, so is their scorn. Associated with the genitals, Scorpios may struggle to separate themselves from their sexy reputation, however private they keep their love lives.

Scorpios are perhaps the deepest of all the water signs and so can require some extra patience and searching to get to the core of their mysterious selves. Scorpios have a negative energy that means that most of their emotions will be kept internal, however, they might like to express their emotions through writing, like Scorpio poet and novelist, Sylvia Plath. This sign doesn't like to allow itself to be vulnerable (remember their rather sensitive associated part of the body) so trust and loyalty may be hard won. This Scorpion is quick to protect themselves and their loved ones from any harm, so may keep their armour up until they decide it's safe to let someone in.

Born in the middle of autumn, Scorpio is a fixed sign that may enjoy security and can be single-minded in their approach towards reaching their goals. Co-ruled by Mars and Pluto, these astrological bodies give Scorpios a controlled and competitive attitude that will generally mean that they end up getting what they want out of life once they set their mind to it; take the three Scorpio Jenners, Kendall, Kris, and Caitlyn, as perfect examples of Scorpio's sexiness, controlling nature, and ability to transform.

THE SCORPION

Terrifying for most people to behold, the venom in their tail perhaps not helping, the scorpion has a fierce reputation that some Scorpios can most certainly live up to. However, there is so much more to this creature than just their sting. Throughout a scorpion's life, it will shed its exoskeleton when it becomes too small and emerge larger and more powerful than before. Scorpios may experience a similar transformation within their lifetime, whether it's shedding their childhood as they move away to university, deciding on a change in career in their later years, or an internal transformation of some kind. Whilst the scorpion and Scorpio go through these changes, they can be at their most vulnerable as their new-found selves fully form. However, once the transformation is complete, both will reveal themselves stronger and more powerful than before. The scorpion is a predatory and defensive creature. Just like a Scorpio, they can go after what they want and are prone to lash out if they feel confronted. A nocturnal animal, Scorpios may also enjoy plenty of partying on nights out in their younger years; find them in the clubs shining under the ultraviolet lights like the mysteriously glowing scorpion!

PLUTO AND MARS

Renamed a dwarf planet in 2006, Pluto co-rules the sign of Scorpio with Mars. Pluto's demotion has made it no less mysterious to onlookers and its secrets are yet to be fully understood, which makes it a fitting ruler for the secretive Scorpio. Named after the Roman god of the underworld, this planet is associated with power and depth, just like the emotionally deep and controlling sign of Scorpio. The measured power from Pluto, teamed with Scorpio's other ruling planet, Mars, makes for a sign that has controlled energy with plenty of drive and fight. Named after the Greek god of war, Mars is linked with passion and can feed into a Scorpio's possessive and sensuous nature. From Mars, Scorpios can find the courage to go after what they desire, both in their personal and professional lives. Born in the eighth house in the zodiac calendar, which is associated with regeneration, the power of Pluto and the strength of Mars mean that Scorpios can hold huge potential for transformation and may choose to reinvent themselves several times over.

ELEMENTS, MODES AND POLARITIES

Each sign is made up of a unique combination of three defining groups: elements, modes and polarities. Each of these defining parts can manifest themselves in good and bad ways and none should be seen to be a positive or a negative – including the polarities! Just like a jigsaw puzzle, piecing these groups together can help illuminate why each sign has certain characteristics and help us find a balance.

ELEMENTS

Fire: Dynamic and adventurous, signs with fire in them can be extroverted. Others are naturally drawn to them because of the positive light they give off, as well as their high levels of energy and confidence.

Earth: Signs with the earth element are steady and driven with their ambitions. They make for a solid friend, parent or partner due to their grounded influence and nurturing nature.

Air: The invisible element that influences each of the other elements significantly, air signs will provide much-needed perspective to others with their fair thinking, verbal skills and key ideas.

Water: Warm in the shallows and sometimes freezing as ice, this mysterious element is essential to the growth of everything around it through its emotional depth and empathy.

MODES

Cardinal: Pioneers of the calendar, cardinal signs jump-start each season and are the energetic go-getters.

Fixed: Marking the middle of the calendar, fixed signs firmly denote and value steadiness and reliability.

Mutable: As the seasons end, the mutable signs adapt and give themselves over gladly to the promise of change.

POLARITIES

Positive: Typically extroverted, positive signs take physical action and embrace outside stimulus in their life.

Negative: Usually introverted, negative signs value emotional development and experiencing life from the inside out.

SCORPIO IN BRIEF

The table below shows the key attributes of Scorpio.
Use it for quick reference and to understand more about this fascinating sign.

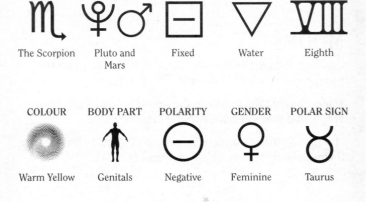

SYMBOL	RULING PLANETS	MODE	ELEMENT	HOUSE
The Scorpion	Pluto and Mars	Fixed	Water	Eighth

COLOUR	BODY PART	POLARITY	GENDER	POLAR SIGN
Warm Yellow	Genitals	Negative	Feminine	Taurus

ROMANTIC RELATIONSHIPS

· · · · · · · · · · · · · · · · ·

When it comes to Scorpio's relationships, there is no dipping your toe in with this water sign – their love is more like plunging head first from the highest diving board. The intensity of sexy Scorpio's affection can be scary for some, and less-daring signs may feel intimidated by their passion, but those that are brave enough to take the plunge will be rewarded with Scorpio's exhilarating and all-consuming love. A Scorpio might make their partners jump through some hoops to test their loyalty, but it's only to see if they are as serious about the relationship as the Scorpio is. Only then will Scorpios really open up to their partners. When Scorpios fall in love it is truly, madly and deeply with their heart, body and soul.

In a long-term relationship, this fixed sign can have a steadfast approach to the one they love; there's nothing fickle about Scorpio's feelings. A committed Scorpio is loyal and protective and will always come to their partner's defence. Potential partners will be attracted to sexy Scorpio's charisma and enigmatic charm, but only the lucky ones will know Scorpio's deepest secrets and feelings as this secretive sign will only share these with a chosen few in their lifetime. Once a Scorpio lays claim to their chosen partner, their passionate love can turn into an obsessive jealousy if they're not careful.

With the influence of Pluto, Scorpios may experience some power struggles in their relationships and with their warring planet of Mars guiding them, disagreements can turn into a battlefield if emotions run high. Possessive Scorpios should try to resist controlling their partner and give them as much autonomy in the relationship as necessary, especially

11

with individualist and free-spirited signs like Aquarius and Sagittarius. Regardless of what has set Scorpio to attack mode, if a Scorpion is arguing with their lover, it is because they think they are worth fighting for. If you are an angered Scorpio or fighting with one, try to turn that intensity into passion rather than rage.

ARIES: COMPATIBILITY 2/5

If it's passion Aries desires in a relationship, a Scorpio could be the perfect sign for romance. However, this match might be too controlling and combative for long-term happiness. Both ruled by the planet Mars, these two may come into this relationship armed and ready to fight. Scorpio's controlling tendencies could be a source of many of arguments. If this fire and water duo can work out a balance of control and ease the Scorpio lover's jealousy, then these two could have one steamy relationship, rather than being left hot and bothered.

TAURUS: COMPATIBILITY 5/5

Scorpio and Taurus are each other's opposites on the zodiac calendar, so cosmically share a special relationship both in their differences and similarities. The element of Taurus is earth and Scorpio's is water, which usually will mean that both partners provide something that the other desperately needs. Love and passion are both driving forces for these two. Scorpio has the reputation for being the sexiest of signs and Taurus the most beautiful, so a physical relationship should be strong here. Whilst this couple will no doubt enjoy each other's bodies, their tendencies towards possession and jealousy will need to be kept in check.

GEMINI: COMPATIBILITY 3/5

Passionate debates could be on the menu for a Scorpio and
Gemini love affair. The water sign of Scorpio will bring
emotional depth to the relationship whilst a Gemini's air
influence will help breathe a fresh perspective on things.
Scorpios risk suffocating Geminis with their intense emotions
if turned toxic. Geminis can be flirtatious, which can trigger
Scorpio's jealousy, but Geminis aren't scared of a little
arguing, in fact they quite like the stimulation. Being a fixed
sign, Scorpios value steadiness so may find flighty Gemini too
unreliable, however, this relationship has the potential to be
full of spice and interest.

CANCER: COMPATIBILITY 2/5

These two water signs can easily get lost in each other's emotions.
Ruled by Mars, Scorpio's passion for their Cancerian lover will
be intense and a Cancerian will likely be highly attracted to a
sensual Scorpio. Both the Scorpion and Crab can be stubborn
and unwilling to bend to their partner's wishes if they don't
match their own. Claws and stingers at the ready, disagreements
could see both sides getting hurt and might end with them
parting ways quickly. However, once these two decide that they
want to be together, they can experience a love that is unfailing
in its loyalty.

LEO: COMPATIBILITY 1/5

The love between water sign Scorpio and fiery Leo can be one of deep intimacy or dampened spirits. Here are two fixed signs that could clash in their different approaches and refuse to yield to each other's strong personalities. Shared assets, particularly money, could prove difficult for a Scorpio and Leo. Scorpio is born in the eighth house where shared possessions are important, and Leos belong in the fourth house where a love of gambling lives, which could result in conflict for the couple. If respect is exercised regularly between these two lovers, theirs is a closeness well worth protecting.

VIRGO: COMPATIBILITY 5/5

Placed two apart on the zodiac calendar, the passionate and loyal bond between the Virgin and Scorpion is a special one. Orderly Virgos will value the steadiness of fixed sign Scorpio, and similarly the loyal Scorpio will appreciate the faithfulness that many Virgos are known for. With their complementary elements of water and earth and their matching negative energies, this typically introverted couple will enjoy the nourishing effects of spending quality time with each other. Theirs is an intimate relationship but not without some passionate arguments, thanks to power-ruled Scorpio's influence of Pluto and Virgo's sharp tongue.

LIBRA: COMPATIBILITY 2/5

When the planets align for Scorpio and Libra, the combination of loving Venus, passionate Mars, and powerful Pluto can make for an intimate and stimulating love affair. The emotions of a water sign and the mindfulness of an air sign can be a harmonious pairing so long as a Scorpio and Libra are on the same page. Librans can seem superficial to the deep-feeling Scorpio, but thankfully when this head-and-heart-ruled couple fails to understand each other, Libra's charm and diplomacy can help calm any troubled waters. This love won't be without conflicts, sorry Libra, but it could be loyal and long-lasting.

SCORPIO: COMPATIBILITY 4/5

Was there ever a couple more deeply and desperately devoted to one another than Scorpio and Scorpio? The intimate connection that these two mysterious introverts can make is both in mind and body. They both can be guilty of passionate outbursts, particularly with jealousy, and their fixed attitudes can lead to arguments if they can't agree. If these two can patiently hold their breath in stormier times, then this is a relationship that could sail off into the sunset together. Scorpio and Scorpio are a true power couple that, thanks to their hardy Scorpion nature, can withstand plenty.

SAGITTARIUS: COMPATIBILITY 2/5

Sagittarius and Scorpio can have a daring partnership; whether their gamble on each other pays off is another thing entirely. The adventurous Sagittarian will help expand Scorpio's horizons and appeal to their brave side, whilst Scorpio's fixed attitude can teach the flaky Sagittarian to stay motivated and see things through. The love of Scorpio can be all encompassing and the worst thing for a Sagittarian is for them to feel like their partner is at all possessive. This is definitely not a boring love, but flexibility and growth are both key for these two getting the most out of the relationship.

CAPRICORN: COMPATIBILITY 5/5

When Capricorn and Scorpio set their sights on each other, these highly dedicated signs could be in it for the long run. Placed two apart on the zodiac calendar, theirs is a devout bond that is likely to be highly compatible with matching negative energies, complementary elements, and harmonising cardinal and fixed modes. A Capricorn can offer the security that Scorpio desires and Scorpio can be the powerful influence that feeds Capricorn's ambition. Scorpio will bring the fun and Capricorn will bring the itinerary to go with it. If they can take it in turns to rule the roost, their love could go the distance.

AQUARIUS: COMPATIBILITY 1/5

Mysterious Scorpio and unique Aquarius may well find themselves attracted to one another, but the Scorpion and water sign Aquarius may need to work hard to keep their relationship off the rocks. Positive Aquarians are outgoing, and socialising in their communities is important, but this contrasts with introverted Scorpios who tend to have a small and intimate circle of friends. Their modes are both fixed which means they can be resistant to changing their contrasting outlooks. If stable Scorpio can embrace this air sign's free-spirited nature and rational Aquarius can provide the intimacy that Scorpio needs, then these two could find their happiness.

PISCES: COMPATIBILITY 4/5

Here are two water signs that will go to the ends of the earth, or rather the depths of the oceans, for one another. Pisceans dream of finding that fantasy love and the enigmatic Scorpio can be just that for them, whilst the empathetic Pisces can be the kindred spirit that secretive Scorpios can finally be vulnerable with. A Piscean's mutable nature, which flows with change, can be at odds with the steadfast approach of a fixed Scorpio, but their differences mean that they have plenty to learn from each other. Emotional security and sensitivity are where these two thrive.

FAMILY AND FRIENDS

. . . .

The negative energy in Scorpios means that this sign is quite happy to spend time alone, however, even if they do not actively seek out new friendships, the bonds that this sign will make are extremely important to them. Scorpio's group of friends is likely to be small as they value quality over quantity. Each friend of a Scorpio will have been carefully selected and may have gone through rigorous tests set by their Scorpion comrade to prove their worthiness. The reason for Scorpio's caginess comes back to their fear of letting their guard down and exposing themselves to pain. Trust is an important practice for any Scorpio who wants to experience the benefits of close friendship.

As with most relationships, whether it be friends or family, finding common interests is key to forming and maintaining bonds. Secretive Scorpions could adore a good mystery, so a day out solving an escape room or a night in discussing this month's thriller book club choice could be two great ways for a Scorpio to bond with their suspense-seeking friends. Virgo's methodical analysis could make them the perfect partner for helping Scorpios get to the bottom of a crime, or an extrovert Leo friend will no doubt jump at the chance to arrange a murder mystery in a spooky house for all of their friendship group to enjoy.

Another passion of sumptuous Scorpio is food and drink, whether it be opening an expensive bottle of wine at home or enjoying the tasting menu at the latest Michelin star restaurant in town. Scorpio's negative energy could have them spending all day at home, whipping up a gluttonous feast for their family and friends to enjoy, who likely will be quite familiar with Scorpio's culinary talents. Venus-ruled signs, Libra and Taurus, are friends that will happily indulge in Scorpio's love for luxury and will probably be the ones bringing over the bottles of champagne to their Scorpio host.

Scorpios can be emotionally intuitive parents; if there is something amiss with Scorpio's child, or any family member, this sign could readily pick up on it and be set on fixing whatever the problem is for their loved one. The Scorpion's love for their family is intense and their protective nature is formidable to challenge, so loved ones should rest assured that Scorpio has their back through thick and thin. The possessive and jealous side of a Scorpio could rear its unsightly head when it comes to those that this sign treasures most. Scorpio will indeed love their family like treasure and they will no doubt be the most valuable thing in this sign's life, but they should avoid treating people like possessions and trust their family to always return to them. Empowering their friends and family rather than using their own power over them will be key in maintaining happy and successful relationships for Scorpio.

MONEY AND CAREERS

. . . .

Being a certain star sign will not dictate the type of career that you have, although the characteristics that fall under each sign could help you identify the areas in which you may potentially thrive. Conversely, to succeed in the workplace, it is just as important to understand what you are good at as it is to know what you are less brilliant at so that you can see the areas in which you will need to perhaps work harder to achieve your career and financial goals.

Committed Scorpios aren't inclined to flit between jobs, unless they are still figuring out what they want to set their mind to. Scorpio's immense dedication may well see them stay in the same job or working for the same company for many years, whether they are 100% happy in it or not. A Scorpio devoted to their career should make sure that it comes from a place of passion rather than complacency. Scorpios can value security above their job satisfaction, and if they fear failure, then they may decide to not try anything too daring. Channelling the influence of Mars, Scorpio should dare to dream and actively chase after their career goals with courage.

Scorpio's single-minded approach to life can mean that they lose themselves obsessively in their work, so it helps if they are passionate about their career. A sign as mysterious as Scorpio will often be attracted to the obscure or shadowy and won't shy away from darker occupations. Whether it's making an indie film inspired by fellow Scorpio Martin Scorsese, writing a thriller novel, or working in a funeral home, what might give other people nightmares could be the Scorpion's career calling.

MONEY AND CAREERS

· · · · · · · · · · · · · · · · ·

Scorpios tend to be very private, especially when it comes to their bank accounts; asking a Scorpio about their salary could feel like asking them to strip down to their underwear. However, it might be clear from Scorpio's lavish spending habits as to how well they are doing financially. High earning jobs will certainly suit the shopaholic Scorpio who enjoys treating themselves to the very best of everything. Remember, this sign is about quality over quantity so whilst their shopping bags may be few, what lays inside them is likely to be of high value. The secrecy around spending and their funds may mean that they choose to keep some of their finances under wraps, even from their spouses.

Whilst you can't always choose who you work with, it can be advantageous to learn about colleagues' key characteristics through their star signs to try and work out the best ways of working with them. Hardworking Capricorns can bring structure and order to the work life of a Scorpio and make sure their passion for a project does not fizzle out before it has reached fruition. Signs with a strong influence of Mercury, like Virgo and Gemini, will offer their thoughts and opinions willingly to a Scorpio seeking advice and can be important colleagues to bounce ideas off.

HEALTH AND WELLBEING

. . . .

The scorpion is known for being able to withstand almost anything. Freeze this creature solid, then thaw it out and this durable wonder can still be alive! Similarly, Scorpios (minus the freezing bit) can endure serious hardship and deep emotional grievances. These folks are certainly made of hardy stock, but their water element can make them feel pain more deeply than most and make their inner power hard to channel at times. Scorpios are undoubtedly strong, but their tendency to isolate themselves in times of stress can sometimes weaken them as they close themselves off to any outside support. This controlling sign may struggle to ask for help and allow their vulnerability to be exposed, but asking for help is never a sign of weakness and should only help strengthen Scorpio.

When a stressed-out Scorpion is feeling overwhelmed, they can turn to escapism for an immediate solution to their problems; bingeing on box sets, wrapped up in a blanket, and wearing their pyjamas may be a familiar scenario. Whilst cocooning themselves away like this may feel initially comforting, they should be careful of doing this too regularly as it could also start to have the reverse effect. Losing themselves in a good book or spending time with an Aries or Leo friend who they have not seen in a while could be a far more positive distraction. Hearing about the problems of others may give some healing perspective to Scorpio's own issues, or at the very least will strengthen their friendship ties and make both parties feel happier from having taken the time to catch up.

Whilst this sensitive sign may be the best of all the water signs at controlling their emotions thanks to the influence of

Pluto, Scorpio's sting of aggression will usually pierce their victim with the strongest of venom. Fortunately for everyone, Scorpion's scorn is usually infrequent, but trying to avoid big bursts of aggression is still an important lesson for this sign to learn. Scorpios can have a wonderful sense of humour, so trying to channel a lighter mood that allows them to laugh at life, rather than going on the attack, will hopefully diffuse any internal aggression from building up. Scorpions are intense by nature and their serious side is dominant, but inviting fun into their lives and not taking things too seriously should help to balance out their moods.

With the influence of Mars and Pluto, Scorpio can have a lot of powerful energy that, if left unreleased, can cause emotional and physical discomfort. Teamwork isn't always a Scorpio's forte, their negative energy and fixed mode lends itself well to working alone. However, a little healthy competition can really fuel Scorpio's energy, so signing up to a running or swimming race could rid Scorpio of their restless energy and set positive goals for them. If it's a surplus of emotional energy that is building up in this water sign, then finding ways to sensitively release what is inside of them is also imperative; writing poems or a novel could be a positive outlet for this emotional sign as well as always seeking out professional therapy if necessary.

Scorpio

....

DAILY FORECASTS
for 2022

OCTOBER

· · · · · · · · · · · · · · · · ·

Saturday 1st

You might take things too personally today and get very down.
Be sure to correspond your feelings with the utmost honesty
and respect for your family unit. You might need to put your
dreams and visions on hold today and go along with the
crowd's agenda.

Sunday 2nd

Mercury turns direct, but you could be in a stalemate situation
with your inner compass. You might need a few more weeks
before you can think clearly or learn about the next steps to
take. Practical activities can help to take your mind off other
worries, but don't overdo it.

Monday 3rd

Today could see a shift in your finances. This might mean that
you speak to the right people who can help you move forward
to success. This will also benefit your relationship and raise
your self-esteem. You may have a revelation which sets the
tone of your next summit to climb.

Tuesday 4th

Issues within the family could be smoothed over now, but only
if you learn to say no to excess duties. This is important for
your physical and mental health. Look at it as a way of taking
care of your own interests and keeping your stress levels down.

Wednesday 5th

Minor challenges can be overcome today with a little help and wisdom from an elder in the family or a leader in your social groups. Your spirits can lift if you're prepared to listen and not resort to radical or temperamental behaviour. Direct your energy into seeking answers from your psyche.

Thursday 6th

Romance and creativity are highlighted for today. You might be switching off and withdrawing into your fantasy world where you can explore the depths of your art and love. You may feel like merging or connecting with others on an ethereal level. Spiritual groups can support your need for belonging.

Friday 7th

Today it's important that you recognise any issues involving communication or study. You might be reaching out or picking up a course where you left off. If you've experienced a mind fog, expect that to be lifted as your discernment kicks in and you sort the good from the bad.

Saturday 8th

You're almost at the end of an old habit or project which is no longer serving you. Get creative and complete this before picking up anything new. You may be guided by your romantic nature to look for another holy grail, but think twice. Taking on another big quest could be futile.

Sunday 9th

Pluto turns direct and relieves some of the pressure you've been experiencing around changes and endings. A full moon highlights your long list of goals and aspirations – which ones have borne fruit. This can teach you not to overload yourself with duties which may impact your health.

Monday 10th

You may feel driven and wish to make some headway in your personal projects now. However, you must give yourself some time to pause and reflect on what has worked for you and what hasn't. Be confident in your abilities to do well. You don't have to prove anything to anyone.

Tuesday 11th

Mercury returns to your private zone and will continue to explore the depths of your shadow. Your mental abilities to process your feelings will be enhanced. Think of this time as searching for the gold you hid long ago. It's time to shine and heal old wounds. Be gentle with yourself during this time.

Wednesday 12th

A partner might help to put some pieces of the puzzle together today. You could be using them as a sounding board, but be careful not to express any negative feelings which have nothing to do with them. An emotional roller-coaster could take you for a ride through several areas of life.

Thursday 13th

Although you may be prepared to go as deep as you dare to find answers, you might have too many options which can confuse you. Try to stick to one track and follow that one through before jumping on another. Your first piece of gold is waiting to be discovered today.

Friday 14th

Your mental energy is highly active today. This is great news for your personal work, but not so great if your family or social groups distract you. However, you are learning how to love and forgive yourself more. Your inner child may need some reassurance and encouragement.

Saturday 15th

Keep up the good work searching your soul, but spare some time to treat yourself. This evening you may be staying in your safety zone as you've had enough excitement for one day. If others try to coax you out, stick to your guns and let them know you're safe and happy.

Sunday 16th

A passing phase could be challenging. It would help if you comforted yourself with what you love to do. This may involve travel documentaries or cooking exotic foods. Nurture both your body and soul. Contemplate what home means to you and protect yourself from invaders of your time.

Monday 17th

Work or another activity might make you feel vulnerable.
You could choose one close friend or relative to talk to and let
off steam in a safe place. Be kind to yourself and know that this
process is showing how courageous you are. Get back in touch
with your creativity.

Tuesday 18th

A powerhouse lights up your darkest corners. If you stay
positive, alert and on task, you could have a revelation. You
might also be so empowered that people take notice of what
you have to say. Be an example for others to follow. This is
your hidden gold showing up.

Wednesday 19th

You may have to be brutal today and lay the law down about
something you're not happy about. However, you can put this
across well enough not to cause friction. Stand your ground if
you're confronted about this. Don't let others push you around
or make you small again.

Thursday 20th

You are becoming a force to be reckoned with. This is evident
today in the way you handle situations at work. You might also
be rearranging finances and getting more control. This might
not be easy, but with perseverance, you can solve any issues.
Unwind with friends and interest groups this evening.

Friday 21st

Today is more easy-going and you can relax. You could be contemplating your relationship and what it is that you share with each other. This could be finances or shared pleasures. Look at this methodically and practically without letting emotions guide you.

Saturday 22nd

Something from your psyche could push its way to the surface today. This could make you feel exposed but can also be a cause for celebration. You may be surprised by how important this is to your self-esteem and wish you'd revealed this talent or dream a long time ago.

Sunday 23rd

Saturn turns direct now, and you may notice the pressure from family members has eased. Perhaps you've set strong boundaries this year and people have more respect for you. You may also have a stronger resolve to take care of your own needs better. The Sun moves into your sign. Happy Birthday!

Monday 24th

A general sense of satisfaction fills you. You you might feel more in line with your inner compass than previously. Not only do you know your limits and have identified where you push yourself too far, but others have realised this too.

Tuesday 25th

A new moon in your own sign lets you set goals and intentions around you and you alone. Venus has entered your sign, too, and can enhance the need to think about your values, self-worth and how you attract beauty and quality into your life. If you want more of this, make a wish.

. . . .

Wednesday 26th

Today might feel a little edgy after the last few days, but this only serves to make you more determined to stick to your convictions. A family member may try to push your buttons and a partner could be asking for trouble. Deal with this knowledgeably.

Thursday 27th

Stay alert for something else coming up from your psyche. It might be small but no less significant to your personal growth. You could be pushing the boat out and being impulsive today, so take care with your spending as it could easily get out of hand. Only do what's necessary.

Friday 28th

Jupiter jumps back into your romantic and creative zone. Is there something you didn't finish earlier this year? Perhaps you have loose ends that need tying up or a forgotten project waiting in the cupboard. Now is your chance to complete this or to make a grand gesture to a lover.

Saturday 29th

Mercury is done digging for gold. It's up to you now to bring it forth yourself. If you wish to take a break from this personal journey, do so knowing you have the tools to pick it back up in the future. Your senses are tingling and desire some intrigue.

Sunday 30th

Your ruler, Mars, turns retrograde today. This period might be the excuse you need not to push ahead with deep and mysterious topics. If you really must pick up a new project, start from the very beginning and use the guidebook. Take it slowly and master it.

Monday 31st

You could be optimistic today, but an air of anticipation hangs over you. This is due to your understanding that shifts are happening and you're not sure if you have control. Keep an open mind and think outside the box. Perhaps your old ways of doing things need a total overhaul.

NOVEMBER

Tuesday 1st

Today is definitely not the day to push ahead. You could be experiencing many triggers from childhood which fill you with self-doubt. This heavy energy suggests that you need to take time to gather your thoughts and resources. Which limits are self-induced, and which can you break through?

Wednesday 2nd

You may be overthinking and getting yourself in knots today. Your physical and mental energy aren't co-operating. Move your focus onto your romantic and creative projects and let out anything you have bottled inside. Old loves and hurts may return to your awareness. Let them go and unburden yourself of this baggage.

Thursday 3rd

Your emotions and deep thinking can be your saving grace today. As your mood lifts you can process thoughts in your own unique way. Think and feel from the heart and you can be more productive and turn overthinking into self-analysis. Remember to be kind to yourself during this process.

Friday 4th

Hold on to your inner compass today. You could be creating something which is unusual for you and will need to play around with it a while. The perfectionist in you might be critical, but the romantic keeps you working until you're satisfied. Don't rush your work, master it.

Saturday 5th

You might have a better idea of what you need to throw in the cosmic waste bin today. This can come as a revelation and can also bring some heartache. Don't project this trauma. However, it's essential that you release this in order to move on and be your best self.

Sunday 6th

A day with the family could be good. There may be a lot of jobs that need doing and a group effort would be effective. You could be leading the way and organising this. Tricky discussions involving the past could occur and these must be concluded, forgiven and forgotten.

Monday 7th

If you feel like indulging with good food and company, make sure that all your daily chores are completed first. You could be more selfish now and wish to do your own thing, but you will come up against a problem if you neglect your duties. Do the responsible thing then have fun.

Tuesday 8th

A full moon and lunar eclipse in your relationship zone could throw a spotlight on what you've achieved. The strange energy can be disturbing and throw you off balance. Listen to your inner voice and refrain from reacting in old unhelpful ways.

Wednesday 9th

Watch what you say as volatile energy can mean that you speak without thinking. There may be issues of jealousy or nastiness within your relationships. You can turn this energy into something more exciting if you play it right. Decision making may be difficult later, so take time to consider the options.

Thursday 10th

You may have to be humble and turn to someone in your family for advice. This might also be an overdue apology. Something isn't fitting right at the moment and you need to get to the bottom of it. Try not to be fooled into wishful thinking or false romantic notions.

Friday 11th

Burning the candle at both ends will only make your health suffer. You might notice this today as your energy wanes and you have trouble doing menial tasks. Your mental processes may be preoccupied with things that aren't important right now. Slow down, rest and prioritise.

Saturday 12th

Listen to what your inner voice is telling you as it's possible that it's communicating with your true North and checking if you're aligned. You might feel out of sync and could do with some nurturing to get back on track. Consider where you feel most protected and why you refuse to allow this for yourself.

Sunday 13th

You might be more sensitive and intuitive today. Use this wisely as you can navigate your way through the day with care and empathy for others. If you feel safe, you can relax and help others to feel the same. Do what feeds your soul and give yourself a treat.

Monday 14th

Stay in your safety zone this morning and come back to that feeling if you feel attacked or vulnerable. What you hide from others is your softer side, but sometimes you need to expose this so you can be appreciated and understood. Find your voice this afternoon and be a leader.

Tuesday 15th

Beware of illusions today. You may have been under the impression that romance and creative pursuits were going well. This could be possible, but there is also a risk that you get drawn into idealistic thinking. Check in with your core values and keep a level head on your shoulders.

Wednesday 16th

The planetary energy suggests that you shift your focus from yourself to your value system. Think about your goals and aspirations. What resources do you have? How can you gather more of what you need? It might be time to restructure your home, finances and personal philosophies.

Thursday 17th

Your friendships may need your services now. You could be in demand or going through a sorting process and deciding which contacts no longer serve your best interests. Be part of a community or group who believe in the same things as you. Don't give your time to those who don't share your values.

Friday 18th

Practical work will be good for you now. Filing, sorting,
making lists and joining in social activities can be helpful.
You might have to put your personal dreams and introspection
to one side and contribute to a group venture or a good cause.
Shake up the system and start a revolution.

Saturday 19th

A quiet weekend is favoured as you might need to process
recent events alone. Put your creative projects aside and
simply put your personal world to rights. You can get a better
idea of what means the most to you now if you use compassion
and research.

Sunday 20th

You might not have the time or energy to blend in with
the crowd today. If you need to decline an invitation, do
so politely and offer them your services for another time.
Alternatively, you may be interested in connecting with
elders and discussing family history to piece together missing
information.

Monday 21st

There may be something urgent to do today. This could involve
putting yourself out there to be noticed. Perhaps you've
overlooked a deadline or appointment. As the moon returns
to your sign you may feel this intensely. Express your desires
this evening. Be honest and open-minded.

Tuesday 22nd

A brief moment of nostalgia or a yearning for past times must be dismissed as this can bring your mood down. It can also induce problems and arguments in your current relationship. Look ahead at what new things you can achieve with the one you love. Aim high and stay sharply focused.

Wednesday 23rd

If you can connect to your inner compass today, do so as a reality check. However, it may still be evading you. Practical, hard work might be an alternative answer. Intense feelings can make you super productive, but this can also exhaust you.

Thursday 24th

Jupiter turning direct and a new moon ask that you seek truth in everything you do. Look at the quality in your life. What holds value for you? What is too materialistic? Perhaps you need to indulge yourself with connecting to the wider world and exploring more. You may be attracted to other cultures and higher education.

Friday 25th

You might need to slow down and use today for minor adjustments. It's possible that there's been a shift and you need to catch up with it. If you hate change, this can be troublesome. Learn to embrace the ebb and flow of what life has to offer.

Saturday 26th

A day of reflection could be good for you. The festive season is about to kick off and you may be too busy for this. Today you might be able to connect with your partner around finances and shared investments. You could be thinking of change with too much emotional attachment.

Sunday 27th

Reconnect with people you've neglected recently. You could win some brownie points if you reach out to a lover and rebuild your relationship. It may have been a tough few months, but you have a chance now to get back on track and co-create a harmonious life together.

Monday 28th

You could be slogging away today at your responsibilities and feel like you're getting nowhere. All you can do is to forge ahead and lower your expectations of yourself. No one is asking for a miracle, just that things get done and deadlines are met. Don't stress too much about this.

Tuesday 29th

Mentally you may be drained today. Unfortunately, you must soldier on until you've completed your work. You may need to be around someone close this evening to let off steam. Find a friend who won't be offended if you speak openly and honestly about your grievances. Let it all out and then breathe deeply.

Wednesday 30th

Let yourself drift today. You could feel lighter after offloading your baggage. Going with the flow can be easier and less of a problem. You may feel that you're a small fish in a big sea, but this doesn't bother you today. A simple day is what you need.

DECEMBER

· · · · · · · · · · · · · · · · ·

Thursday 1st

Don't let anything rock your boat today. You might be adrift and switching off, but outside influences continue to nag at you. Hold on to your inner compass, but remember that not all is as it seems right now. Stay calm and centred and let the outside world pass you by.

Friday 2nd

You may be more optimistic today and can come back to mundane life with a smile on your face. This break might have boosted your health and strengthened your constitution for the upcoming festive season. Do what's necessary and look forward to a weekend with exciting plans.

Saturday 3rd

It's likely that you're extra busy now and can breeze through your day with strong motivation. You might be inspired to spend on luxury goods or connect with others from far away. Reach out to people you have neglected lately and plan for an evening of swapping stories.

Sunday 4th

Neptune turns direct now. You could begin to see things more clearly and get an upgrade in your artistic and romantic endeavours. Be careful that you aren't clinging on to a dream that wasn't meant for you in the first place. Let it go and seek a new perspective. Partners can be supportive now.

Monday 5th

Put your best foot forward and extend your gratitude to someone special. You may not have the chance again. Big projects may be coming to completion and you should feel proud of yourself as this might give you a place in the wider community. Excitement or restlessness fuels you.

Tuesday 6th

You deserve the good things in life. If they're offered today, grab them with both hands. This could mean a jump start to get your dreams manifested. Your emotions may run deep, but your mind can be more grounded and help to anchor you. This is a great starting point for adventure.

Wednesday 7th

Enjoy a day free of difficult energy. You may be returning to your deep and personal inner work, but remember that your ruler, Mars, is still retrograde in this section, so lower your expectations and take things slowly. Look around, survey the territory and learn what you're dealing with.

Thursday 8th

A full moon highlights what has been going on for you regarding shared investments, learning, teaching and researching. Financial matters could come to a head and may need urgent attention. You may also have a revelation regarding your inner workings and the darker corners of your psyche.

Friday 9th

You may feel insecure today and could do with gentle chats and words of encouragement. Look to maternal figures who can offer this and take extra time to listen to what they say. Your emotions may be larger than usual, and your concerns could be out of proportion. Let yourself be looked after today.

Saturday 10th

Loving words and harmonious communication can be a source of comfort today. You might realise that the long road of personal development is never-ending but worth every step. Commit yourself to undertake this quest and make it your goal to be kind to yourself along the way.

Sunday 11th

If you begin to feel vulnerable or exposed today, look at your achievements this year. Someone needs to tell you that you've worked extremely hard and have accomplished a lot to be proud of. Come out of the shadows and shine. Let yourself be seen and heard because you are worthy of success.

Monday 12th

It could be time to reach out to family members and offer them gratitude for their support this year. You may also be seeing the bigger picture and be thankful for the lessons you've learned about maintaining healthy boundaries. Group ventures and family matters can also be celebrated.

Tuesday 13th

Some irritation is possible today, but you must refrain from using selfish or boorish behaviour to get your own way. This phase will pass, and you must respect that others have their own stresses to deal with too. Use up your restless energy in another way, such as exercise or planning.

Wednesday 14th

Today you could be the go-to person for your social activities. As you're good at organising, you may be called upon to host an event which can be fun and adventurous. Put pen to paper and brainstorm your ideas now. You can be imaginative but practical at the same time.

Thursday 15th

Great earth energy can ground your ideas and help them to grow. These may be short or long-term and you don't have to hurry to meet deadlines. Surprise yourself by setting a pace that you're unfamiliar with and be guided by it. This can be much slower than you're normally used to.

Friday 16th

You could be ignoring your personal dreams today as what you're doing for the moment is more important and time-consuming. This doesn't mean that your own agenda is forgotten about, it simply means that you are prioritising what needs to be done. Reconcile yourself to this later.

Saturday 17th

You may have a conflict of interests now and a pang of regret that your own path has been side-lined. Don't worry too much about this. Use your mental energy to get through the next few weeks. Surprise someone special with an unexpected phone call or message this evening.

Sunday 18th

Balance your own needs with those of your family unit today. There may be jobs to do or plans to be made with your friends. This could interfere with your rest time and you might need to withdraw if it gets too much. Stay in control as tempers could flare up today.

Monday 19th

The moon in your sign intensifies the atmosphere and insists that you put every effort into being your best self now. This could mean that you've let things slide a little or put your energy into what's not so important. Hard work and dedication will make the day go quicker.

Tuesday 20th

Jupiter bounces back into your health and duties zone. This can be a great sign for your health, but as Jupiter expands everything he touches, you must remember not to take on too many responsibilities. If you must, then try to have fun.

Wednesday 21st

The winter solstice arrives with the shortest day. This could make you feel rushed to get your workload done. However, you should pause, reflect and reward yourself for the past year. This evening you might wish to switch off and snuggle into the winter nights ahead.

Thursday 22nd

Your one-to-one relationships might need attention today. Expect the unexpected and you may have a lovely surprise. Try to involve family members in the planning for the festive season. Don't take it all upon yourself. You could easily get emotionally overwhelmed, become unfocused and make mistakes. Ask for help or delegate duties.

Friday 23rd

A new moon in your communication zone can help to make your mind up about what you wish to pursue for the coming year. This is likely to include study, research or networking with others. It can also be something which will take a lot of time and energy.

Saturday 24th

Today the air is filled with anticipation. There may be many messages or visits to make before bedtime. However, there should be no hiccups as the planetary energy is favourable and even romantic. Your words and desires match your deeds and you can create beauty in anything that you do today.

Sunday 25th

Your family life is blessed with love, altruism and humanistic attitudes today. Prepare yourself for a fun-filled day with much joy and laughter. However, you could overdo the good things, so be careful. Your circle may pull together to make this a truly great day to remember.

Monday 26th

You may need to relax today and not do very much at all. It could be that you indulged too much yesterday and are regretting it today. You should lie low and do as little as possible. Show the younger members of the family what it takes to be responsible and respectful.

Tuesday 27th

Today you can relax more and do your own thing. You may not have too many duties to do and can drift off into your own fantasy world. If you choose to spend time with a lover, you may have a dreamy time and be reminded of your shared visions for the future.

Wednesday 28th

There are blessings available for you if you know where to look. These may be your sense of adventure and willingness to try new things. Your inner compass calls you and if you check in, you might see that a compassionate way of communicating is winning you bonus points.

Thursday 29th

Mercury turns retrograde today. Just as the year ends, you are reminded to back up devices, double-check travel plans and be more mindful with your speaking and listening. You could feel an instant effect of this today and you will need to be extra careful with your planning.

Friday 30th

Tiredness could set in today, so don't do anything over and above the necessary. You may have some thoughts about your personal path, but now isn't the time to pursue this, so keep it on the back burner until after the holidays are over. Make plans in your head for next year.

Saturday 31st

There is a lot of challenging energy around today. You could be rebelling against your duties or suffering with your health. Either way, you might not be in the mood to party. You may wish for something more intimate with a loved one.

Scorpio

....

DAILY FORECASTS
for 2023

JANUARY

. . . .

Sunday 1st

Start the new year by having a deep conversation with someone important in your life. As a Scorpio, you often favour soulmate connections over superficial chit-chat. If you are thinking of someone you used to know, reach out and get in touch. Make a New Year's resolution to let go of regret.

Monday 2nd

When it comes to love and relationships, there's no rush. Use this period as a time to re-examine your own feelings. Consider what you want and what's important to you in your one-to-ones. Give yourself a few weeks to think things through before taking decisive action.

Tuesday 3rd

The planet of connection, Venus, enters Aquarius today. This is a time when home and family affairs dominate, but in a way that's potentially productive and collaborative. If you want to get on the right side of someone in your family, or regarding a property issue, here's your opportunity.

Wednesday 4th

If you've become fascinated with an esoteric subject or metaphysical knowledge over recent months, your fascination is likely to continue for another few months. This may be a deep period of learning for you when you're willing to push back boundaries to explore the secrets of life.

Thursday 5th

Your close relationships may continue to delight and excite you, even though there might be nothing stable or conventional about your love life. Think of a relationship as a journey that reflects who you are and is a steep learning curve. Be experimental in your one-to-ones.

Friday 6th

Today's full moon could be a reflective or questioning time for you. What you think you knew may be challenged, or your beliefs could shift and change. A conversation you're involved in or a book you read might be the spark that reignites the activist side of your nature.

Saturday 7th

It's an excellent weekend to join in with a course of study or a workshop. Allow the full moon energy to expand your life and explore a different direction. What you hear or discover could enable you to set off on a new path, one that may awaken profound wisdom and deep learning.

Sunday 8th

What you experience this weekend could remind you that not everyone gets who you are. That's okay if you know your best friends are people of like minds. Who you want to hang out with might be changing. A political or social difference could be a stumbling block in a relationship.

Monday 9th

Make an effort to get back on track with someone close to you. This could be a member of your family or a romantic partner. Venus and Mars, the lovers of the heavens, are connected today, encouraging you to find your counterpart, the person you feel most at home with.

Tuesday 10th

If it's becoming a challenge to pursue your path in life, take a look at your past or your family relationships. There may be a reason why you can't do what you want now and your priorities lie elsewhere. Or, perhaps you're not feeling as confident as you usually are.

Wednesday 11th

If you meant to get back in touch with a friend or colleague over the festive period, but it didn't happen, it's a good time to try again. Send a short text or email and reach out. You don't have to write a long essay explaining everything that's going on. Start by opening the door.

Thursday 12th

Your ruling planet, Mars, turns direct today after ten weeks in retrograde. This is about inner power, strong emotions and the conviction that what you're doing is right. There can be no turning back now. Decide what you want to do and why and be assertive in your actions.

Friday 13th

Mars is back up to speed in your joint finance and shared resource zone. This is about money and the power that money holds. If you've been waiting on a payment or you're involved in a battle over money, it's a positive indication for you. Try again where you failed previously.

Saturday 14th

Take some time out this weekend if you know it would help. If you're typical of your star sign, you often benefit from peace and quiet in your life, time to think and explore. You may enjoy sorting things out at home or hanging out with a member of your family who knows you well.

Sunday 15th

A love relationship could be unpredictable now. At least, it feels as if things aren't settled between you and someone close. Other people may behave erratically, so don't make up your mind about another person based on what you witness. Step into your power later on today.

Monday 16th

You may start the week feeling out of sorts if a relationship is more off than on. It may help to take a step back so you can get a broader perspective on what's happening. New information might come to light in a couple of days which could help reveal more.

Tuesday 17th

The moon is in your star sign until the evening. Make the most of this and put yourself first. Spend some time considering your personal goals and aims and draw up a wish list for your next steps. Other people will be more attracted to you now. Use your magnetism to good effect.

Wednesday 18th

Mercury turns direct in your communication zone today. This can act as a green light when the truth emerges and new information is revealed. It could help you make an important decision that you've been putting off since before the holidays. It might entail saying no.

Thursday 19th

It's a promising time to get back in touch with someone who's gone quiet on you. This might be a sibling, a neighbour or a member of your local community. Be proactive and sort out any problems or issues that have been dragging on. Reopen the lines of communication.

Friday 20th

You might be drawn towards the past when someone gets back in touch with you, perhaps online. You may be exploring your family tree or want to reconnect with distant family. It's a good weekend to consider your home and where you live and make some plans for the future.

Saturday 21st

Today's new moon takes place in Aquarius. This is promising for new beginnings, whether you're moving home, changing things around where you live or you're thinking of new ways to utilise your home. Start your initiative to rent a room, find a lodger or organise a party or get-together.

Sunday 22nd

Don't keep to yourself but reach out to other people, whether you're healing old wounds or craving more connection. Visit an elderly relative or catch up with someone you haven't seen in ages. This isn't the time to try and sort out a romantic relationship as the ball is in their court.

Monday 23rd

If someone from your past or a family member doesn't want to see you, let things be for now. It's never easy when a close relationship reaches a stumbling block, but be accepting of their needs. When the time is right, you'll get another chance. Try to be patient.

Tuesday 24th

Tap into the artistic side of your nature and consider how you can bring your creativity into your work or your daily routine. It's a good date to spend quality time with a child if you're a parent. Keep life light and don't underestimate the art of conversation and making new friends.

Wednesday 25th

If you want to work from home more of the time, this would be a good date to put in a request. There's a little bit of luck linked to home and family affairs, your work and your health. The more smoothly your routine works for you, the less stressed you'll be.

Thursday 26th

Jupiter, the planet of opportunity and growth, is in your work and health zone. This would be a great time to line up some new fitness goals and take a small step towards optimum health. Keep repeating a habit until it becomes an automatic part of your daily routine.

Friday 27th

Love planet Venus moves into emotional water sign Pisces today. This could be romantic for you and it would be a gorgeous few weeks for dating. Notice who comes into your life and look out for the person who's kind and caring. Prioritise your close relationships.

Saturday 28th

You can't keep everyone happy today, so choose your companions carefully. It's a lovely time to be around your children if you're a parent. Or, hang out with a friend who is sweetness personified. Stop giving yourself a hard time and be open to compliments and gentle reassurance.

Sunday 29th

Your star sign has a reputation for being sexy and seductive. You may have been on an unconventional journey in recent years when it comes to love and relationships. Freedom remains a key feature for you, but don't take this too far or detach from your feelings.

Monday 30th

It's an excellent date for communication and getting to know someone new on a deeper level. If you want more passion in your life or you're open to finding love, be proactive and take the first step. If you're exploring your sexuality and you're open-minded, experiment more.

Tuesday 31st

You could be keen to step out of your comfort zone today and explore a new direction in life. This might be linked to money, sexuality, personal growth or transformation. You could have an experience of being a mind-reader or be closely tuned in to your psychic powers.

FEBRUARY
· · · · · · · · · · · · · · · · ·

Wednesday 1st
Your imagination may be in overdrive today. This is good news if you work in a creative field. Otherwise, you could easily lose yourself daydreaming and your thoughts or online ventures could lead you down more than one dead end. Deal with something practical at the very least.

Thursday 2nd
It's a lovely day for being around people or meeting up with your friends. If you've been spending too much time recently at work or lost in study or reading, reconnect with your emotional intelligence. There's still a lot to learn but in a more connecting capacity.

Friday 3rd
You may find it harder than usual to concentrate today, especially if you're juggling a lot of different balls at home and at work. It might take longer than expected to get hold of the relevant people and some conversations could run away with you. Pace your schedule accordingly.

Saturday 4th
Someone close could let you down this weekend. There may be a rift or split in the family, someone who doesn't want to see you. Try not to overreact to other people's actions and, when in doubt, be open-hearted. It might help to lose yourself in your work or a creative project.

Sunday 5th

The lovers of the heavens, Venus and Mars, clash today. This can flag up a battle of the sexes, so try not to let yourself get triggered. The full moon lights up your career zone. You could step into a new job or different role where you're able to shine brightly.

Monday 6th

Use the full moon energy today to reconsider the work/ life balance. You may see your situation with clarity and recognise where you need to put in more time and where to do less. Rather than give yourself a hard time, firm up your commitments over the next few weeks.

Tuesday 7th

It may not be the best time to tell a good friend everything. If you reveal too much about love or money, this could work against you. For starters, you may react badly to what they say and an argument could flare up quickly. Some confidences are best kept secret.

Wednesday 8th

If you have feelings for someone, let them know today. It would be a wonderful time to sign up to a dating app or express your emotions. Enjoy flirting and having fun. If you're not in the love game, reach out to a child or grandchild and initiate a spontaneous conversation.

Thursday 9th

Slow things down today and you'll get more done. Prioritise what's important rather than what's urgent and you'll find you can achieve more. You may benefit from some quiet time to think things through, especially if you know you have to make a big decision coming up soon.

Friday 10th

Talking is a serious matter, whether you're doing it for a living or you have to be careful about the words you use. You might be talking in a court of law or be writing a thesis that has to be accurate. Either way, communication could feel painstaking or plain hard work.

Saturday 11th

Communication planet Mercury enters your home and family zone today. This could be helpful for negotiations or getting things sorted where you live. If there's someone in your life you know would benefit from a close conversation, reach out to them.

Sunday 12th

The moon is in your star sign Scorpio today, which means you're the one in charge. If you want to change your plans and cancel a date or social event last minute, be decisive. Someone close may be disappointed, but it's the right time to prioritise your health and your stress levels.

Monday 13th

The more you set clear boundaries in place at home and within your family, the easier you make things for yourself. Caring for an elderly parent could be exhausting if you're trying to do it all on your own. Get other people involved, whether that means your family or a professional.

Tuesday 14th

Money and work could take centre stage today, which isn't great news if you were hoping for a romantic Valentine's Day. The best time for you to enjoy a romantic encounter would be tomorrow lunchtime. This is when your stars are positively fizzing with romantic possibilities.

Wednesday 15th

Take note of one of the most romantic planetary combinations of the year that takes place at lunchtime today. It's an ideal time to open your heart and you may intuitively know what you want when it comes to love. Someone in your life could declare their affections for you.

Thursday 16th

Home and family matters could feel heavy or slow you down today. It's here where the pressure's on, whether you're dealing with a serious family issue or you're stuck in a familiar situation and can't find a way out. Get more support on your side if you think it would help.

Friday 17th

Keep talking if you're unsure how to handle a home or family issue. A third party or another family member may have an unusual answer or a quick way to resolve things. Don't keep your feelings bottled up and acknowledge any stress you're under. Start by being kind to yourself.

Saturday 18th

You may find you're swept along on a wave of emotion today as the Sun enters Pisces. If you're in the midst of a love affair, it may feel overwhelming and deeply romantic at the same time. It's a wonderful time to prioritise your hobbies and talents.

Sunday 19th

The day before the new moon is traditionally a time to rest and retreat. It would do you the world of good to have a day at home, even if you are sorting out a few financial matters. This evening, there's a stunning planetary line-up that promises romance and a soulmate connection.

Monday 20th

Today's new moon could see someone new sweeping into your life. It could feel like a fantasy, but that doesn't mean you can't still enjoy yourself or embrace a wonderful experience. This is potentially a lucky time for you. Embrace play and fun, entertainment and good times.

Tuesday 21st

If you want to become a parent, this would be the ideal time to declare your intentions to the universe. This week's new moon highlights children in your horoscope. Alternatively, this could also apply to the things in life that you give birth to, including a creative masterpiece.

Wednesday 22nd

If someone let you down yesterday evening, don't let your feelings get in the way of reaching out and reconnecting. Once you dig a little deeper, this may reveal what's going on. You might be acting in a new role as therapist today, whether you're with a good friend or a work colleague.

Thursday 23rd

Team up with other people at work today, socialise together or get the right person on your side. Put fresh energy and impetus into your everyday life and your working routine. This isn't a time to go it alone. Ensure you have people around you who are not only helpful but fun as well.

Friday 24th

Don't be a loner in life and reach out to others. This is important both in your place of work and in your social life. This evening looks gorgeous for getting to know someone close a whole lot better. Give in to romance and do something special with the one you love.

Saturday 25th

You may sense an impulse or desire to act fast when it comes to love and partnership. Ring the changes and this could benefit a relationship, especially if you've been stuck in a rut of late. It could work the opposite way, however, and someone close does their own thing.

Sunday 26th

If you're a parent, you may notice where this holds you back today. Try not to let the kids come between you and your other half. Ensure that life isn't all work and no play. If you want to spice up your love life and recharge your relationship, go for it this evening.

Monday 27th

If you're looking for work or you want to increase your worth, this could be a good day for negotiations or making new contacts. It's not all about you, however, so work alongside your team or reach out to the right expert. Then, you could end the day with more support.

Tuesday 28th

Use your words and vocabulary wisely and be aware that your wicked sense of humour or cutting cynicism may not do you any favours today. You might have to explain yourself when someone doesn't understand your behaviour. Make an effort to listen more than you talk.

MARCH
....

Wednesday 1st

It's a wonderful day to come up with some new and brilliant ideas for your next steps. Whether you're planning a holiday or trip away or you're committed to a course of study, expand your experience of life. Using visualisation techniques could help you turn a dream into reality.

Thursday 2nd

Your work or your health could get a welcome boost today. What happens may lift your spirits when you hear good news about a job or health situation. Listen out for a compliment or congratulate one of your work colleagues. Be firm regarding a home or family issue.

Friday 3rd

Communication planet Mercury is now in water sign Pisces. Therefore, this would be a lovely weekend for an intimate conversation. Be empathic towards other people but take a step back from a situation you can't control. Someone may ask you to be a listening ear.

Saturday 4th

You can go far when you get the right people on your side. Work alongside a team of creative people to ensure that a new project gets the best possible start. If your other half asks you to drop your plans for them, this isn't a good sign. Put your projects and ambitions first.

Sunday 5th

It may be the weekend but the moon is currently in your
ambition zone. Therefore, if you put your mind to it, you
could come up with a clever idea that earns you good
money. Get back in touch with your power and channel your
determination into a new work goal.

Monday 6th

Go for it today and take a leap of faith, whether you're
planning a family, falling in love or being a creator. Great
events only materialise when you're willing to take the first
step. Also, consider your everyday routine, what works for you
and what changes may be necessary.

Tuesday 7th

Today's full moon cuts across your social and romance zone.
Therefore, this is a good time to get back in touch with friends
and meet up with other people. It's important to put firm
boundaries in place around love or regarding your children.
Enjoy yourself but don't get carried away.

Wednesday 8th

You may be taking a long hard look at what you do in life that
brings you enjoyment. Notice when you feel disappointed and
where you lack commitment. If you want to master a musical
instrument or become an artist, prove your dedication and
start putting in the hours.

Thursday 9th

Slow down the pace over the next couple of days. You might be delegating your work or handing over a role of responsibility to another team member. Keep your vision and faith strong even if you feel under the weather or you don't have the energy to get much done.

Friday 10th

Try not to be overly worried if you've had to let go of a work activity or postpone an exercise goal. Your turn will come. Sometimes, you just have to give in and rest. There may be an opportunity this weekend to get back on track with a personal aim or project.

Saturday 11th

If you're typical of your star sign, you don't always like to ask for help. This weekend, you could do yourself a favour by teaming up with other people to make your job easier. Partner up, whether you're cracking on with a work project or you want a gym buddy to give you accountability.

Sunday 12th

The moon in your star sign may give you an extra boost of confidence. Yet, that doesn't mean you're going to win over everyone to your way of thinking. Steer clear of the person who insists on playing devil's advocate. Hanging out with kids is a sure-fire mood booster.

Monday 13th

Do yourself a favour and get an early start. Double-check you have payment options to hand and don't get caught out when a child tries to slow you down. It's a good day to be optimistic about money. If you've got a goal, crack on with your plans.

Tuesday 14th

Be savvy with your money. Listen out for new ideas and keep things fresh on the financial front. Also, try not to let other people seduce or scam you. Use your common sense to discern who's right and who's wrong. Keep your cards and your cash close to your chest.

Wednesday 15th

Focus on where you can quickly bring about change. Pursue a financial investment or contact someone in a position of power or influence. Work alongside a partner to further your interests and try not to be overly impatient. This evening is perfect for romance or an art or music event.

Thursday 16th

Love could hit new heights today as love planet Venus enters your relationship zone. Wear your heart on your sleeve and try not to let money get in the way of love. You may have to lay down the law in the office if someone holds you up or you're asked to work late.

Friday 17th

You may choose to say less not more today, perhaps because you're ill informed or you haven't done your research. You might be undergoing a period of intense study and have a lot of commitments that require you to step up. Keep juggling the work/life balance as best you can.

Saturday 18th

Talk things through with your family or people at home today. Create a timetable or a new system that helps you live together well and benefits everyone. Keep your eye on your work and routine even if it's the weekend. Ask someone close to change their plans to suit you better.

Sunday 19th

Communication planet Mercury enters fiery Aries today. You may turn into a motor mouth. It seems you have a lot to say and you're ready to act fast. It's a good weekend for creating more structure or organisation in your life. Leap into action and don't hang around.

Monday 20th

Learn to delegate over the next few weeks. When you manage people well, this can help you save time and energy. The equinox heralds the Sun's move into Aries when life often speeds up fast. Get busy with your work and routine, your lifestyle and your health.

Tuesday 21st

This week's forward-moving astrology takes place in your work and health zone. You may be unusually busy now with a lot to do and different projects to juggle. Today's new moon in Aries is perfect for setting some clear intentions and boundaries.

Wednesday 22nd

Channel your energy into holistic self-care. Set some clear goals around fitness, time management and lifestyle factors. Be your own life coach and take steps to boost your energy levels and your mind-body-spirit connection. The fitter you feel, the more you get done.

Thursday 23rd

You may take a journey into the past over the next few weeks. There could be a reason why you're spending more time with your family, your parents or someone you grew up with. There may be a theme of letting go, whether you're shedding possessions or selling a home.

Friday 24th

You might not feel in charge today as others could take the lead. Ensure you have people around you who keep your feet on the ground and that there's someone you can turn to, a person who's your rock. This is important if you're dealing with grief or a loss.

Saturday 25th

Your planet Mars leaves Gemini and your joint finance zone today after seven long months in one part of your horoscope. This could coincide with a property sale or a financial contract that comes to a close. Start to look to the future and reorient your gaze away from the past.

Sunday 26th

Lay down new rules or guidelines around money and spending. This may be important regarding your relationship with a child or lover. If finances are tight, get other people on board to stand alongside you and change any expensive habits together. A new job could be perfect timing.

Monday 27th

If you're looking for work or you're keen to apply for a new job, don't hold back and act fast. This week is brilliant for new initiatives that could turn your life around quickly. Sign up to a coaching session, go back to school or rewrite your CV. Use your networks to help you.

Tuesday 28th

It's a great day to ask for what you want at work. You might be negotiating holiday pay or to get holiday dates in the diary. Be pushy if necessary. The more confident you are, the more this could rub off on other people. Start a healthy eating plan or initiate a new fitness goal.

Wednesday 29th

Line up some fun and games and make sure that you're not alone in doing so. Decide who your dream partner is for your next big adventure and enrol them into joining you. A person with an infectious spirit and a lust for life could reawaken your passion and desire.

Thursday 30th

Your one-to-one relationships might be a great source
of excitement and awakening over the next few weeks.
Alternatively, you may realise who's moving away or where
change is required. Love could take off fast today. A couples
holiday might be on the cards.

Friday 31st

Be true to who you are, even if you're not sure where you're
heading or how to deal with new developments in a close
relationship. Remember that as a Scorpio, you have the
emotional strength not only to survive but thrive. Dig deep
and explore life to the full.

APRIL
. . . .

Saturday 1st

Love may feel like a tug-of-war game today. You might be yearning for a soul connection while the one you're after is making a bid for independence. Or, perhaps it's the other way around. Either way, work and career are in the ascendancy whilst your relationships look unpredictable.

Sunday 2nd

If you've been extra busy at work recently or you've been caught up with your fitness goals, readdress the balance of life today. The moon's move into your friendship zone is a clear indicator that people matter. Drop some of your commitments to spend time with friends.

Monday 3rd

You may be obsessing over your partner or an ex today. Or, perhaps you realise you can make swift progress when you team up with a coach or adviser. It works both ways, so look at where other people can benefit you and where you're giving too much of your time and energy away.

Tuesday 4th

Ensure you keep clear boundaries within your relationships. Try not to let a friendship become overly flirty and make sure your partner knows what is and isn't okay within your partnership. Plan a quiet night at home this evening and catch up on some much-needed alone time.

Wednesday 5th

Full moons tend to heighten emotions. You may find that everyone feels slightly on edge during this mid-week period. It would be a good day to talk to a child or make a decision regarding children. Here, you can make progress and be the voice of wisdom.

Thursday 6th

Today's full moon highlights work and routine, lifestyle and health in your horoscope. It's about what you do on an everyday basis and how you take care of yourself and others. You may draw up a new schedule. Or, listen to your inner voice and know when it's time to retreat.

Friday 7th

The moon's back in your star sign today. Make the most of this and have a productive start to the weekend. Draw up plans with your children if you're a parent. Or, with a lover, if you're enjoying a relationship. Don't leave things to chance as a romantic evening beckons.

Saturday 8th

It's an excellent day to talk about long-term plans if you're in a romantic relationship or business partnership. Whether you're booking a holiday or creating a new wish list, keep your gaze on your future goals and what's next. Someone close may have to reschedule your date or get-together.

Sunday 9th

It's not the best day for relationships or seeing eye-to-eye with the one you love. You may have different ideas about love. Or, you want or need different things from the partnership. Keep close tabs on spending too. Aim to teach a child how to budget well.

Monday 10th

It could be a great day for being extravagant, whether you're shopping or enjoying some pampering or treats. The more optimistic you are about money matters, the more you attract abundance into your life. Be open to receive or send a gift to the one you love.

Tuesday 11th

The planet of connection, Venus, moves into your joint finance zone today. Lean on other people to share your resources and offer your advice to a family member. If you're a typical Scorpio, you're savvy about money matters. Step into your power and take charge of finances.

Wednesday 12th

It may take a while for a job win or positive health result to sink in. Try not to underestimate what's happening and pat yourself on the back if you've played your part. A spontaneous conversation could lead to an exciting conclusion, whether love or a teaching role is the result.

Thursday 13th

Not everyone will be keen to celebrate your good news, so be discerning who you share the information with. You might rejoice getting into a school or course of study. Or, perhaps you're a parent and your child is the one who's done well. Put your feet up later on.

Friday 14th

You might have to step in and advise a family member today. If they're having a love or money crisis, start by calming them down and be the voice of reason. If you're in a marriage or long-term relationship, it might be your turn to step in and support your other half.

Saturday 15th

If you don't want someone visiting your family or coming round to your home, lay down the law first thing. It will make a big difference to how the rest of your day goes. If someone close requires a boost of confidence or their spirits lifted, do your best to put a smile on their face.

Sunday 16th

If you're talking to a child about a holiday or study option, make sure you can deliver what you promise. Don't get involved in a game of social one-upmanship trying to outdo your ex or another parent. In a similar vein, keep your dreams realistic and not beyond your reach.

Monday 17th

Be a dreamer today in the best possible way. Take a step back from your daily routine and try something new to stimulate the creative or spiritual process. It might be a walk in nature, a leisurely swim or good deed for a stranger.

Tuesday 18th

It's back to the drawing board today as you attempt to implement new ideas or plans into your routine. You might not get it completely right at the first attempt but make an effort to embed a habit into your lifestyle. If it makes you feel good, you're on the right track.

Wednesday 19th

Lucky Jupiter continues to bless your work and health zones. This is where opportunity lies, so broaden your experience in both these areas. It's an ideal time to take a risk, have a big vision and use your power of self-belief to make things happen. Be expansive in your approach.

Thursday 20th

Look back to the equinox and what you started on or around March 21st. There may be another chance to get this right, whether it concerns your work, your health or your fitness. Today's eclipse could signal an ending in your working life which brings about a new beginning.

Friday 21st

Communication planet Mercury turns retrograde today in your relationship zone. Sometimes, people go quiet on you during the Mercury retrograde phase. Other times, you're the one who wants to take a step back. Don't leap in and try and fix things. Be patient and more willing than usual.

Saturday 22nd

There may be a financial impact on your life if someone
has taken a retrograde step. Whether there are changes to a
romantic relationship or a business partnership, consider what
this might mean for your earnings or financial situation.
Keep the lines of communication open.

Sunday 23rd

There's a possibility that someone may step in to help you
today. You could receive a gift or a compliment. Or, perhaps
the one you love shows their generous nature and kindness of
spirit. Love and emotions may be tangled up with money and
finances. If so, practise fairness.

Monday 24th

You could go back on your word today. Or, perhaps someone
close changes their mind about a holiday you were planning.
It's not the end of the matter by any means so try not to
overreact to another person's indecision. Consider any way
you can work towards a joint resolution.

Tuesday 25th

You may have some tough negotiations on your hands today.
Or, perhaps you're aware it's time for a serious conversation
with a child or partner. Whatever you're up to, be realistic
about what you can and can't achieve together. Don't over-
promise and work within your limitations.

Wednesday 26th

If you want to go on holiday or have an adventure, you could consider taking a solo experience. As a Scorpio, you're fearless and independent so this doesn't faze you. It might not be typical, but it doesn't mean you have to give up your dream.

Thursday 27th

There may be a clash between your work and career, your home and family life today. Plans could change suddenly first thing and you feel bad leaving someone in the lurch. Decide where your priorities lie and what's most important. Not everyone will agree but do what's right for you.

Friday 28th

You may have to rise to the challenge today if you encounter opposition to your plans. You could be up against someone at work who has different ideas to you. Or, perhaps you meet someone socially who's outspoken and not in agreement with you. Hold steady with your beliefs.

Saturday 29th

It might be hard to let someone down but actually, you're letting them off the hook. There is a difference. Your independent move could be just what they need to break free. In effect, you're doing them a favour by staying true to who you are and following your agenda.

Sunday 30th

A good friend may be keen to meet up as they've got a lot to tell you. You might not be in the mood to get together or perhaps you're feeling tired. Yet, make the effort and it will be worth it. One of your favourite activities is an intimate heart-to-heart.

MAY

. . . .

Monday 1st

You may be transported back to events that took place during the Equinox or towards the end of March. A sense of grief or loss could feel overwhelming, so ensure you have someone to talk to. Reach out to your other half or find an expert who knows what you're dealing with.

Tuesday 2nd

You might feel a bit lost today and want to hide away. If you're holding on tightly to a personal grievance, this could be the time to release it and let it go. This month's lunar eclipse falls in your star sign, which may be a powerful turning point.

Wednesday 3rd

If you want to cancel a social event this evening, go for it. It's important that you do what's right for you and not let other people call the shots. Ideally, you'll be working at home today or have some quiet time to mull things over. Try not to take on too much this week.

Thursday 4th

You don't have to keep delving into the past. If you want to close a door and stop reliving an experience, be firm with yourself. Once you relax and let go, you may find that you can more easily concentrate on the present and start to think about future plans.

Friday 5th

A powerful eclipse is taking place and you're wise to listen to your inner voice and let your emotions speak. Events that began in October 2022 may come to culmination during this period. Dig deep to reach knowledge or gain insights that have lain dormant for some time.

Saturday 6th

Being a Scorpio, it is often your most intimate connections that define who you are. You love nothing more than being with another person on a soulmate level and trying to uncover what's hidden. During this powerful eclipse weekend, make the right kind of connections in your life.

Sunday 7th

The planet of love and connection, Venus, moves into your travel zone today. If you recognise that it would be good for you to get away or go somewhere different, make it happen. If you're in a relationship or married, talk to your partner about going on holiday or taking a trip.

Monday 8th

Don't miss out on a job or contract that could earn you good money. Keep your eye on the ball regarding work and financial matters this week. You might have been sidelined by a personal matter but a new opportunity won't be around forever. Take decisive action before mid-May.

Tuesday 9th

There may be a chance to turn the page and start afresh in a personal relationship or professional partnership. Today's events could bring the unexpected. If you're single, you might meet someone new. It's a lively time for love when being spontaneous could make a difference fast.

Wednesday 10th

You could experience a tricky encounter today when it seems as if you're talking to someone from an opposite viewpoint. There may be a language barrier or a political difference that's exposed. Try not to let this get in the way of your work and take a step back if necessary.

Thursday 11th

Communication planet Mercury remains retrograde until Monday 15th. Any challenges within a personal relationship could reappear now and leave you feeling confused. You pride yourself on reading people on a deep level but even you may not know how to help someone close. Be patient.

Friday 12th

A child in your life requires consistency and needs to know where they stand. Therefore, it's important that you and another parent or guardian are reading from the same page. Bring a new level of commitment to your closest relationships and ask for the same in return.

Saturday 13th

Shift the balance in a close relationship if you've been dealing with some heavier issues recently. Make a concerted effort to keep things light this weekend and have some fun with the ones you love. You could make an agreement that certain topics are not to be spoken about.

Sunday 14th

Put work to one side and ensure you enjoy the weekend. Actively engage with one of your favourite hobbies, hang out with your kids or a lover. The more time you spend doing what you love, the more fulfilled you feel. Find a sense of peace and calm in your life.

Monday 15th

There's a strong pull on your emotions now. Or, there may be someone in your life who's a strong attraction. This person could be good for you or lead you astray, so be discerning who you spend your time with. As Mercury turns direct today, now's the time to talk.

Tuesday 16th

Unleash your inner romantic from today as lucky Jupiter enters your relationship zone. This could offer you a chance to find happiness in love and enjoy your personal relationships to the full. It's about getting your love situation right so it works for you and the other person.

Wednesday 17th

Jupiter rules freedom as well as opportunity. Therefore, if you're in a relationship that's not working out, you may have a chance to fly free and break away over the next few months. It's not just about love – find your ideal business partner, therapist, coach or teacher.

Thursday 18th

Ensure you have good people around you. You could be feeling lonely for a partner if you're single. Or, perhaps you're apart from the one you love. If you're grieving a loss or are feeling sentimental about the past, ensure you have support life.

Friday 19th

Today's new moon falls in your relationship zone. If you're in a relationship or married, do something special with your other half. In all close relationships, both personal and professional, this offers you an opportunity to close a door on the past, turn the page and start afresh.

Saturday 20th

Intensity is starting to build this weekend as your planet Mars enters your career and vocation zone. This is an indication that you're wise to turn your attention to your future goals and next steps. Make some bold and audacious plans.

Sunday 21st

You could make an all-or-nothing decision this weekend that not only impacts your home and family life but your future path too. It might be linked to what's happening in your partner's life. Or, perhaps you're the one who's not ready to settle down as you're craving freedom.

Monday 22nd

This week, you may be ready to change things around and set off in a new direction. You may not know exactly which way to go, but choose at least one path to commit to. Turn your focus to work and money matters, as it's here where you can make an ambitious move.

Tuesday 23rd

It's never easy when your decisions affect people close to you. That's not a reason, however, to stop living the life you choose. If you have a chance to perform on stage or take on a new role as boss or CEO, it's a no-brainer. Step into a pair of new shoes.

Wednesday 24th

When you make a decisive step about your future, you move one step further away from a challenging situation. This is likely to be a good thing, as it means you're less attached and freer from past expectations. There may be some sadness involved but keep your eye on the prize.

Thursday 25th

Not everyone will agree with what you're doing, but don't let that hold you back. You don't have to apologise or try and explain why you're making the choices you are. Sometimes, you get a calling in life and, when the voice is strong, you know you have to respond.

Friday 26th

The moon remains in your career and vocation zone today calling you forth. Unexpected support or praise could delight you, especially if it's from someone who means a lot to you. If a partner wants to book a trip away or do something spontaneous this weekend, say yes.

Saturday 27th

Make the most of the long weekend. If you're in a relationship and the two of you could benefit from some time together, make it happen. This could mean reorganising some things, but you have to do what's best for the both of you. Make a pact that love will prevail.

Sunday 28th

There could be a temporary disappointment today regarding money. You might have to lay down the law with a child or lover if they're not being realistic around their finances. If you're the one who needs to rein things in, don't avoid what could be a painful decision.

Monday 29th

Put yourself and your needs first today. That might mean postponing a get-together with friends or arranging to do less, not more. It could benefit you at the end of this momentous month to take some time out and reflect on recent events. Seek the calm spot in your life.

Tuesday 30th

You may have come across a new topic recently that's fascinating. If so, this would be a great time to learn more. Buy a book or read some articles online. If you're exploring a subject linked to life beyond the veil, the esoteric or metaphysical realm, you're in tune with your stars.

Wednesday 31st

Recharge your batteries and restore energy levels today. It would be perfect if you're on holiday or on a retreat. You might require some alone time now, which could mean disappointing someone close. Ensure that self-care is a priority.

JUNE
. . . .

Thursday 1st
Don't assume that everyone is in sync with you today or reading from the same page. The moon in your star sign might boost your confidence, but that doesn't mean you can win everyone over to your way of thinking. Being overly enthusiastic or superior to others could work against you.

Friday 2nd
Make a point of listening to what other people have to say, both at work and at home. You may not agree with another person's opinions, but they'll appreciate being heard. There's a romantic vibe later on and it may be linked to a person in your life who lives abroad.

Saturday 3rd
This weekend's full moon brings a chance to shift your money mindset. Your values could be realigned in a good way. Ensure you balance your head and your heart when making decisions. Engage your instinctual nature, knowing where to invest your money, time and emotions.

Sunday 4th
You may be discussing what comes next with a loved one or partner today. Certainly, it seems as if big plans are afoot regarding a relationship or your desire to travel or study something new. It's an excellent weekend to firm up an agreement that ties you and a third party together.

Monday 5th

The planet of connection, Venus, joins your planet Mars in your career zone today. This might mean that you have a new boss or a new work colleague joins the team. For some reason, this might not be to your liking. You may want them to leave immediately.

Tuesday 6th

It's an excellent day for meetings and all forms of communication. You have the gift of the gab and there's a chance to sort out a recent misunderstanding. Get on the right side of a person of influence and you could do yourself a big favour. Enjoy gossiping with a friend.

Wednesday 7th

If your partner's been turned down for promotion or they're having political issues at work, be there for them. The situation may not seem that important to you, but for them, it matters. Do your best to understand another person's point of view, however odd it may seem to you.

Thursday 8th

You could fall out with someone at home today, especially if you've been spending a lot of time at work recently. Try to find a middle ground, rather than be too extreme, and that applies to both parties. Agree to disagree. At best, find a compromise that works for both of you.

Friday 9th

It's a gorgeous day for relationships. If you're a parent and you're seeking quality time with a lover or your other half, make sure the kids have a sleepover. Once you start opening up to the one you love, the conversation could run and run. Share your hopes and dreams with one another.

Saturday 10th

If you're feeling uncomfortable about a financial issue, it's important to explore it a little deeper. You might be putting off a holiday or adventure because you don't want to spend any money. Look more closely at what's going on and see whether fear is triggering your misgivings.

Sunday 11th

Your co-ruler Pluto moves back into your communication zone today. This represents intensity, deep thinking and a psychological shift. An inner process is taking place, transforming who you are. Look after yourself on all levels and endeavour to be your best self. If in doubt, go in deep.

Monday 12th

Turn your attention towards an issue that could be thought of as taboo. This is primarily about money, legacy, inheritance or debt, power or control. Sexuality gets a look in too. Bring your psychological depths and your powers of perception into all areas of your life.

Tuesday 13th

Dare to venture into unknown territory and confront any inner demons. Life's urging you to engage with a difficult or sensitive issue and to reclaim your power in a way that's authentic and genuine. Be aware that not everyone will respond well to your inner therapist coming out.

Wednesday 14th

Align yourself with the right person today and you could go far. This may be a teacher figure or someone with influence and persuasive power at work. Try not to upset someone and be careful with what you say. Be generous and giving to others.

Thursday 15th

Notice your inner desires. Are you yearning for a soulmate connection, intimacy or a deeper understanding of someone close? If you're in a relationship or married, it may be your partner who's keen to unravel secrets from their past and engage with their inner work.

Friday 16th

Talk to a child or lover if they're currently dealing with an emotional or financial issue. Help them put clear boundaries in place. Sometimes, it's hard to say 'no', but that might be what you have to do now and what's best for everyone concerned.

Saturday 17th

The planet of responsibility, Saturn, turns retrograde today. This could coincide with a shift in your personal life, perhaps involving a parent or someone older. You may choose to do things differently to prioritise your children. Or, change things around to protect your emotions.

Sunday 18th

Today's new moon is an excellent date to initiate a money-making project or deal with a financial transaction. New moon energy is proactive and forward-moving. Make the most of this and crack on with a project that helps you financially. This might be linked to your home or family.

Monday 19th

Life's calling you forth to take on a new position of responsibility. This may be regarding a child, becoming a parent or guardian or taking on a senior role caring for others. If you're in a relationship or married, you could be ready to move towards the next level of commitment.

Tuesday 20th

You might be writing or reading detective or horror novels. Or, perhaps you're interested in a taboo issue. If you're a typical Scorpio, you get drawn towards the dark side. This could be an excellent period for self-analysis or healing others. Don your detective hat.

Wednesday 21st

The Sun's change of star sign lights up your future path during the solstice. Give yourself time to dream and visualise what's next and light a candle or burn a fire in honour of this unique time of year. Prepare yourself and get ready to embrace change, rather than try to resist it.

Thursday 22nd

It's heating up in your career zone, whether you're having a passionate affair with someone you work with or your work life is hot for other reasons. You might create a brilliant new partnership that works well on all levels. Get the right balance of skills and you're unstoppable.

Friday 23rd

Are you making plans to travel, study, deepen your beliefs or find meaning and purpose in your life? If yes, you're in flow. Play around with new ideas and new ways of being. Go somewhere you've never been before this weekend, especially somewhere with a view or close to the sea.

Saturday 24th

Be open to looking at your life from a fresh perspective. Any kind of coaching or learning could help you gain fresh insight and it's a positive time to remain open-minded and curious. Step out of your comfort zone and embrace adventure, ideally with someone close by your side.

Sunday 25th

If you're a typical Scorpio you have an incisive mind and this is a good time to use your perceptive brain. Read between the lines, encourage someone to open up and don't be fooled by what you see or hear. Keep talking and the truth will emerge.

Monday 26th

Today's astrology is feisty and suggests a clash or fall-out. You could experience some challenges in a close relationship or business partnership. Be courageous and bold but don't over-react. Be ambitious without thinking you have to convince everyone else about what you're doing.

Tuesday 27th

Take a step back if the week began with a bang. Try and make amends if someone's upset but don't go in all guns blazing. The more gentle and understanding you are, the more chance you have of reconciliation. If you're talking about a holiday or trip away, the timing's perfect.

Wednesday 28th

Potentially, you're in a position of strength or power today. Other people will listen to what you have to say and it will be easier for you to get your point across. But, remember you can't make someone else happy in your life if you don't know how to make yourself happy first.

Thursday 29th

If you're a parent, this is a good time to firm up travel or holiday plans with your children, if you're not heading off already. Children benefit from commitment and stability, so keep any promise you make to them. The same applies for another parent or guardian. Read from the same page.

Friday 30th

The spotlight is turning towards your travel and study zone. You may be dreaming about future goals and how to expand your horizons. This would be a wonderful weekend to set off on holiday or sign up to a workshop or course. To revive a relationship, try something new together.

JULY

· · · · · · · · · · · · · · · · ·

Saturday 1st

It's potentially a lucky day for love and relationships. If you're in a long-term relationship or married, one of you could win a holiday in a competition or a weekend away. Love has a foreign theme, so embrace new cultures and experiences, whether you're single or coupled up.

Sunday 2nd

It's not the easiest of days if you're around someone whose behaviour is unpredictable. You may have to change plans suddenly because of another person's actions. A top tip today is to keep your money in your pocket and not be persuaded to part with your hard-earned cash.

Monday 3rd

Today's full moon highlights education, communication, travel and broader horizons. It's about your beliefs, your philosophy on life and your knowledge and understanding. You may not agree with everything you hear, but events that take place may offer you a chance to stand firm.

Tuesday 4th

There may be some opposition to your plans today. If you're keen to travel or study, you could hear conflicting opinions about what's right and what's wrong. Sometimes, you have to be resolute and determined to get what you want. Step into your power and do what's right for you.

Wednesday 5th

Relationships could bring a frisson of excitement your way over the next few days. It's not always easy trying to reach an agreement with family or loved ones but give them your full attention. Try to look on the bright side and see the glass half full rather than half empty.

Thursday 6th

Don't shy away from a big personality at work. You may want to stay at home and not get involved, but that's not the answer. Up your game and be equally powerful. Relationships come and go but that doesn't mean you can't learn a lot from them.

Friday 7th

A big conversation may be looming in your personal or professional life. If you're involved in teaching or public speaking, face any fears head-on. Remind yourself that you have a lot of wisdom and expertise to share with other people. View any new role as a learning experience.

Saturday 8th

Love and fantasy go hand in hand. Therefore, this could be a wonderfully romantic day. Or, perhaps you're content to dream about that someone special. Sometimes, you benefit from taking a step back from your everyday routine. Immerse yourself in a creative or escapist activity.

Sunday 9th

Tap into your dreams today and line up new experiences. If you're enjoying some time away or you're in unusual surroundings, this could stimulate ideas that open up a new path in your life. Read books, dive deep into movies and have conversations that inspire your wish list.

Monday 10th

Words have power and you may want to speak up for others now or expose an injustice or wrong-doing. Alternatively, you could be unable to get through to someone in a position of authority. Issues around power and control could peak. Breathe deeply if your authority is being challenged.

Tuesday 11th

This could be an exciting time for you, whether you're lining up a meeting or interview, or you're involved with a new project at work. Alternatively, you may be thinking that you need a wider selection of people and friends in your life to help you fulfil different needs and roles.

Wednesday 12th

A conversation or something you hear during this mid-week period could stir your interest. This is a key time for communication, insight and understanding. Another person's intervention may spark a sudden move on your part. Be open to new ideas, alternative thinking and new age vibes.

Thursday 13th

You don't have to hang out with people or friends who agree with you all the time. Being around alternative thinkers and individuals who oppose your ideas could be refreshing and revelatory. Widen your social circle now and dare to push back the boundaries of knowledge.

Friday 14th

Embrace new opportunities in all areas of your life. There might be a chance to travel or study soon. This is a key weekend to explore adventure and new experiences even if you're unsure where you're going. Set off on a journey without knowing where it will lead.

Saturday 15th

Be bold, take a step out of your comfort zone and explore new vistas and destinations. This could be going to a new city or country. Alternatively, you may be keen to study a subject that's always fascinated you. Say yes to learning and adventure.

Sunday 16th

When you have the right teacher, you gain the learning that's right for you. There's so much information and knowledge in the world but it matters most when it touches you deeply. Don't lose yourself in words. Instead, find the person who can deliver the message you need to hear.

Monday 17th

It's potentially a proactive and forward-moving week for you. Think about progress and keep your eyes on your future path. Today's new moon could bring a significant turning point for a holiday or course of study. Decide what stays and what goes. Clear the decks and allow new energy to sweep in.

Tuesday 18th

You might be thinking about someone who lives abroad this week, perhaps someone who would benefit from your advice or guidance, or someone you would like to reconnect with. If so, this is a good time to reach out and get back in touch.

Wednesday 19th

It's an excellent day to be ambitious and share your creative ideas with other people. Stay one step ahead of the game and you're more likely to grab the attention of an influential person. Alternatively, you may be the one who's stepping into the role of influencer – and rightly so.

Thursday 20th

You might be dealing with a situation that weighs upon you. Perhaps a child or lover is struggling and you want to do your utmost to help them. Be realistic about what you can achieve and encourage them to take one small step at a time.

Friday 21st

Tempers could flare if you're unimpressed with a friend's behaviour. Notice what this triggers within you. You may experience a sense of being powerless or be unable to help, which is your worst nightmare. Do what you can but don't expect miracles. A small win is more realistic.

Saturday 22nd

This is a good weekend to dig deep to uncover any truths that have been hidden from you. Chase up any correspondence or ask again if you're waiting on an answer to your question. Be persistent. A conversation could reveal information that's been missing for some time.

Sunday 23rd

There's a stop-start feel to the weekend's events. An event or trip away could be cancelled or postponed. Alternatively, you might have to change your plans because of what's happening at work. The likelihood is that you're going to be busy over the next few weeks.

Monday 24th

You could get caught up in a power game with a person of influence. Be aware that when Venus turns retrograde, someone could let you down and there's a secretive or hidden theme. This isn't the time to be drawn into anything that smacks of corruption.

Tuesday 25th

Venus retrograde in your career zone could symbolise a passionate affair with someone you work with and you both decide to take a vow of silence. These are intriguing times when you won't want everyone to know what's going on. Keep your wits about you over the next six weeks.

Wednesday 26th

The moon is in your star sign giving you a boost of power and confidence. Yet, keep your cards close to your chest, especially at work or regarding your career plans. Not everyone has your best interests at heart. Use your intuitive powers to feel your way forward.

Thursday 27th

You must find a confidante now, someone you can trust. This is likely to be linked to your working life, your career or your vocation. One conversation mid-afternoon could prove revealing. You may discover who's working against you. Keep a close watch for a secret enemy.

Friday 28th

Try not to spend a lot of money or give your money away now, even if someone is very persuasive. Communication planet Mercury enters your friendship zone today, so lean on other people and find your soulmates. It could be an excellent time to join a new group or network.

Saturday 29th

It's a good weekend to reassess your spending habits and consider your savings options. Even putting a little money aside every week can make a huge difference in the long run. Turn your gaze towards your future goals and gain inspiration from a powerful role model.

Sunday 30th

If you're craving real conversation, it's an excellent day to make new friends or catch up with old friends. If you're typical of your star sign, you love nothing more than an in-depth heart-to-heart with your best mate. Widen your social circle and stimulate your clever brain.

Monday 31st

Strong earth sign energy is great for making friendships that last. It's positive for recognising loyalty in your life too and which friends make the cut. You don't usually get on with everyone but your best friends will be by your side forever and a day. Trust works both ways.

AUGUST

. . . .

Tuesday 1st

Look out for the person who you can impress or who can help
you take centre stage. Align yourself with the right people
and you could make swift progress. There may be a big event
taking place today, whether you're celebrating with family,
moving home or letting go of the past.

Wednesday 2nd

Aim to lay down some firm guidelines around friendship or a
group project. If you're spending too much time trying to deal
with issues in these areas, take a step back. Try not to upset
the ones you love today because you're caught up dealing with
administration problems.

Thursday 3rd

It would be easy to get frustrated if someone you know keeps
making the same mistake over and over. It may not matter
what you say if they're not ready to listen. Be prepared for
disappointment and resolve to try again at a later date.

Friday 4th

Tempers could flare quickly today. Be careful that you're not
trying to push your agenda on another person. It's not easy
if someone close won't take your advice, especially a child
or lover. However, it may be worth trying a different tack.
Put your feet up and relax this evening.

Saturday 5th

It may be the weekend, but you could be raring to go and on fire with enthusiasm. Whether you're catching up with work, doing the daily chores or you're on a fitness mission – being active is where it's at. This could help take your mind off a relationship issue.

Sunday 6th

Work your way through your to-do list one task at a time. If you're feeling overwhelmed with a big project, break it down into smaller more manageable items. Consider whether you'd be wise to delegate some of your jobs or chores. It's an ideal day to find the help you require.

Monday 7th

It's potentially a successful time for you when you may be stepping into a new role. Be wise and get things organised and established sooner rather than later. You may be aware that you're going to have to step up your game and take charge.

Tuesday 8th

You can't do everything on your own now and it's not wise to try. There's strength in numbers. When you find the right business partner, a joint venture could take off big-time. Seek an entrepreneur who's working on the cutting edge of your trade and team up.

Wednesday 9th

You may have responsibilities or duties to attend to today that aren't going to be easy, especially if they impact other people's lives. If one person keeps letting you down at work, it's a clear sign that they're not reliable. It may be time to look elsewhere for help and support.

Thursday 10th

When you get the right people on your side, everything else slots into place. A good friend could give you valuable advice on how to handle a tricky work relationship. You fare better when you have people around you who are trustworthy and responsible. Accept nothing less.

Friday 11th

Don't believe everything you hear today, especially around money or love, as someone could be trying to pull the wool over your eyes. They may be deluded themselves and are passing on false information. Keep your wits about you and use your savvy insight in all your relationships.

Saturday 12th

Line up a special event and take a child on a big adventure. If you're a parent, it's an ideal day to prioritise your offspring and spend quality time with them. If you don't have children, put some time into your creative skills and talents.

Sunday 13th

Love could reach heady heights now. Your stars suggest an encounter with an ex, a flame that burns bright for someone from your past. One area that's a no-go is an affair. It would be a dangerous game to play with Venus retrograde in your career zone.

Monday 14th

It's not the best day to bring your personal problems into the workplace. If you didn't sleep well or you're dealing with disappointment, this could impact your performance at work. Try and compartmentalise the different areas of your life and deal with what's most important first.

Tuesday 15th

It's all going on at the peak of your horoscope over the next few days and this could be a significant time for your career or future path. If in doubt, focus on your goals and put one foot in front of the other. Don't waste energy on what's happening in other people's lives.

Wednesday 16th

A venture that starts on or around today's new moon could take off fast. New moons are perfect for setting your intentions and launching a new idea or project. However, other people are involved and more so than you may realise. Get ready for someone else leaping in.

Thursday 17th

Line up a strong support system in your life, both at work and home. It's going to make your life so much easier if you engage with experts, listen to their advice and have a strong team around you. Don't dismiss what someone tells you because they're older than you.

Friday 18th

It may be hard to know who to trust or get advice from now. This is an ongoing theme at present as you flip between listening to someone younger and returning to an old source of information. Ideally, take in all different ideas and use the ones that speak to you.

Saturday 19th

If it's hard to see the wood for the trees, make a concerted effort to do less not more this weekend. You could be disillusioned or feel let down in some way. You may want some time to yourself to nurse your wounded pride. Focus on self-care and prioritise your well-being.

Sunday 20th

The moon remains in the most hidden zone of your horoscope. Therefore, it might be hard to find much get-up-and-go over the next couple of days. Tie up loose ends today but don't commit to starting something new. Approach the person who will listen to you with no judgement.

Monday 21st

Ease your way into the working week. There's no rush and you'll get more done if you adopt a slower pace. If you can fit in some pampering or me-time, make it happen. Go into work late, or book a massage or beauty treatment this evening.

Tuesday 22nd

It can take you a while to forgive and, in some cases, you never forget. Try and let go of old emotions today and release them. Take things one day at a time and don't aim to rush ahead. Appreciate the small moments, the little things and practise gratitude daily.

Wednesday 23rd

The Sun's move into your friendship zone highlights networking and connections. Therefore, don't go it alone when it comes to your work and plans. Instead, get involved with a group of people and support and encourage one another. A friend or colleague could go quiet on you.

Thursday 24th

Communication planet Mercury is retrograde in your friendship and group zone. This isn't the time to make a big decision regarding these areas of your life. Also, you may have to be super patient if one friend is distant or acting out of character. Be there for them and bear witness.

Friday 25th

It's a good time to lean on your team or ask for help from your friends or colleagues. Turn to anyone who can help you feel connected and more established in your current role or what you're trying to achieve. Dig deep today and get back in touch with your ambition.

Saturday 26th

Your stars are urging you to make the most of the long weekend. Slow things down and aim to do less not more. Having a big lie-in would be a great way to recharge your batteries. Later in the day, make sure you're around people who get who you are.

Sunday 27th

You may sense some sadness or wounding at present if there's a problem surrounding a close friendship. Protect yourself if necessary by taking a step back. Mars' move into Libra indicates you need some quiet and solitude. Relaxation or a meditation course could benefit you now.

Monday 28th

It's a great day to catch up with your family and make time for one another. Ideally, there'll be an opportunity for you to engage in some one-to-one conversations, which suit you better than a big social gathering. Superficial chit-chat is rarely your thing.

Tuesday 29th

Your relationships could be volatile and unpredictable today. Alternatively, they could be exciting and adventurous. It goes both ways. Notice which person brings what qualities into your life. One thing your love life isn't right now is stable and steady. Instead, it's a time to embrace change.

Wednesday 30th

Be wary of criticising other people or yourself today. You could have a lively set of friends in your life, which would be fun. Or, you may have too many demands on your time. You might sense that you're out of balance in your life. Be aware of this and act accordingly.

Thursday 31st

This promises to be an emotional few days because of the full moon in Pisces. Surrender to your emotions without becoming overly maudlin or dramatic. You may benefit now from releasing what you're feeling, whether through having a good cry or getting something off your chest.

SEPTEMBER

·················

Friday 1st

Be wary if you have an addictive nature during this week's full moon. Immerse yourself in art, poetry, music or a spiritual path and practise compassion instead. This would be a good time to step into a volunteering role. You could find salvation in helping other people.

Saturday 2nd

A new romance could come into your life unexpectedly over the next few days. An ongoing relationship may be on the verge of a turning point, so be patient. Continue to be there for your other half if they're going through a tough time. Prioritise your love life.

Sunday 3rd

More than any other star sign, you can have a deep and complex inner life. This could prove to be challenging as you're not afraid to venture into dark unknown places. Your willingness to go in deep may surface today so try not to exhaust yourself in the process.

Monday 4th

It's a day of unique turning points. What happens on or around this date could be momentous for your love life. If you've been waiting for someone emotionally unavailable, your opportunity could arise. In all your relationships, there's the potential for something special to happen.

Tuesday 5th

Don't hold back in affairs of the heart. If there's someone you care about deeply, be spontaneous and let them know. A business partnership could prosper now too, especially when you team up with a person who knows a lot more about technology than you do.

Wednesday 6th

If you're worried about a friend or someone you know through a group you're involved with, it's a lovely and connecting day to reach out. 11:11 is a unique moment in time. Notice who gets in touch with you close to this number. Keep things light, however, and don't be too intense.

Thursday 7th

Don't feel guilty if you want to spend more time on your own rather than be around other people. Trust your emotions and do what feels right. You may choose to do yoga at home or meditate. It's your inner life that's both rich and complex and where hidden insights can be found.

Friday 8th

Today's lucky Sun-Jupiter combination hints at good news for a friend and a reason for a celebration. If you want to join a group or you hear about a social occasion that's right up your street, reach out to others, ask for an invitation and you might make some new friends.

Saturday 9th

The social feel-good vibes continue into the weekend. Make the most of this and be around people who expand your life rather than limit your opportunities. You may be helping people this weekend or be around people from a different culture and background to yourself.

Sunday 10th

Whoever you're spending time with today, it could be an intense experience. You may encounter temptation and hidden desires. It's a fertile time to learn more about your passion and what drives you. This evening, do whatever's necessary so you're ready for work tomorrow.

Monday 11th

An influential role model may be back in your life. This is a good time to get on their right side and use your charm and magnetism to win them over. When it comes to your career or vocation, it's not what you know but who you know.

Tuesday 12th

You can't always choose your boss or your work colleagues. Yet, you can decide who you're going to win over and who you're going to take a step back from. Be discerning when it comes to your work relationships as they currently make a huge difference to your status and reputation.

Wednesday 13th

Join in with other people today, whether this is to help your endeavours or to further a good cause. Chase up an old contact or reconnect with a network of people in your life. Not everyone will want to help you, but don't let one rejection stop you from reaching out.

Thursday 14th

Tomorrow could bring a turning point in your life. Therefore, if you've been waiting to hear from someone, don't delay and get back in touch. It's a similar scenario if you're on the waiting list for a group, club or society. Ramp up the charm today and get yourself noticed.

Friday 15th

There's a double whammy of forward-moving planetary action in your friendship zone today. Mercury turns direct and a new moon takes place. This spells good news for a friend or a group project. Press the green light on a community venture.

Saturday 16th

You may be acutely aware that you can't do everything on your own. It's via other people and your connections where you can be more successful and make an impact. If someone wants to get to know you, it's worth being spontaneous and making time for them.

Sunday 17th

Other people continue to open doors for you. This could be in different areas of your life but career and group activities are most likely. Love could get a welcome boost, too. If you've been holding a candle for someone you work with, promising developments could take place.

Monday 18th

You're back in charge today and you may be feeling more confident because of the support you've recently enrolled into your life. Reach out to the person who can help you nail a deal, land a job or get in front of your dream customer. Talk yourself into a strong position.

Tuesday 19th

Keep your feet firmly on the ground today, pay close attention to the facts and discern what's true and what's not. You need a firm anchor in your life so you don't drift off or lose yourself. Find your escape and your bliss but do so in a way that's not detrimental to you.

Wednesday 20th

Align yourself with the right people. Anyone who's controversial or unpredictable could bring you down with them. Gently steer yourself towards the person who's held in high esteem and commands respect. If you have to make a tough decision, it's a good time to do so.

Thursday 21st

If you want to make an impression on someone or be persuasive, this is a great day to go for it. Be authentic and real. This isn't the time to fake it or pretend you know more than you do. Be brave and bold in your interactions and encourage other people to open up.

Friday 22nd

If you want a confidence boost today, remind yourself of your skills, talents and natural abilities. This is a better strategy than asking someone else to raise your esteem. What they say could end up disappointing you, even if it's not intentional. You know when someone's being insincere.

Saturday 23rd

The Sun's move into Libra today highlights the most hidden zone of your horoscope. Traditionally, it's a time for rest, retreat and inner preparation. You may want to spend more time alone, perhaps in deep thought or busy with a project. Listen to your inner voice and trust your intuition.

Sunday 24th

You might end up in a therapeutic role today. You could be ready to reveal secrets from your past or you have listening ears for someone else. If there's something you want to say to a sibling or a neighbour, tell the truth and get to the bottom of an ongoing issue.

Monday 25th

Today's stars are great for making firm plans for the future and looking ahead. Take up an opportunity to step into a position of authority or land a teaching role. This may prove to be a good strategy in the long run. Be the first to congratulate a friend on their success.

Tuesday 26th

You might experience a sense of deja-vu today as you run into the same old issue with someone you love. However much a person might want to change, it's what they do that counts. If you're willing to give them one more chance, go for it but only until the end of the month.

Wednesday 27th

You may be stepping into a parenting role today or be a carer for someone in a position of need. When it comes to your personal life, put a child's requirements first before your own. A new relationship could bring you into contact with a step-family or adopted child.

Thursday 28th

Whatever you want to create or bring into the world, there are two distinct stages. Firstly, visualise your dream and use creative tools to inspire you. Secondly, engage your sense of responsibility for your wish list and take practical steps to manifest your dreams into reality.

Friday 29th

Take some time out or a step back, especially if you have a super busy schedule. It's important that you take care not to overdo things and watch your stress levels. Today's full moon is ideal for making an important decision around your working life, your health or your fitness.

Saturday 30th

If your love life is chaotic, find time today to talk to someone about it. This could be your other half but more likely it will be a good friend or a relationship expert. Work out what you want to say as there may be an opportunity to speak up over the next few days.

OCTOBER

. . . .

Sunday 1st

When it comes to love and relationships, make sure that you're reading from the same page. If you have opposing wants and needs, it may become obvious that the relationship isn't going to work long-term. If commitment is important to you, let the other person know.

Monday 2nd

Be around people in your life who are encouraging and inspiring. The people you spend the most time with will determine how you feel. Reach out to other people today and work on creative collaborations, both personally and professionally. When it comes to romance, keep it real.

Tuesday 3rd

You may have a significant role to play within a friendship or a group activity. If you're typical of your star sign, you're not afraid of voicing the things that are left unsaid. This might mean venturing into taboo territory. Be willing to take a firm stance on the truth.

Wednesday 4th

Listen to your head and your heart before making any decision. The more balanced you are inside, the easier it is to do what feels right. When you make the right move, your mind acknowledges you're on the right path. Everything comes together seamlessly in perfect union.

Thursday 5th

If you're interested in the esoteric or obscure, you could be ready to dive deep into a period of learning over the next few weeks. You may want to be more introspective so you can listen to your inner voice and intuition. Follow a spiritual path that's calling you.

Friday 6th

If there's someone you'd like to get to know better, invite them to go away with you this weekend. If that's not appropriate for you, a day trip somewhere different would fit the bill. If you're looking for love, you're most likely to find it abroad or in a place of study.

Saturday 7th

It's an ideal day to ring the changes and not fall into a routine. Wake up early for starters and seize the day. Try not to read too much into events as your penetrating mind could lead you into trouble. You're wise to keep life light and walk calmly down the path of least resistance.

Sunday 8th

If you're working today, you're in tune with your stars and if you're thinking about next steps, you could come up with some brilliant ideas. Try not to let anger get the better of you as it would be easy to flare up and speak your mind. Keep your private thoughts to yourself.

Monday 9th

Today's stars aren't great if you're prone to giving yourself a hard time. Be kind to yourself now and don't put great demands upon yourself. This is a time for exploration rather than forging ahead. Don't put up with bad behaviour and steer clear of a volatile or out-of-control person.

Tuesday 10th

Do your best not to give all your energy away. Trying to juggle things so everyone gets a piece of your time could prove overwhelming. If in doubt, prioritise the people who need you the most. This may include a friend who's hit a crisis in their marriage or relationship.

Wednesday 11th

Consider what's changing for you and whether there's a theme of rebirth that's powerful. Your co-ruler Pluto turns direct today in your communication zone. This could coincide with a power shift or be the boost you need to propel you forwards. Some secrets can't be kept hidden.

Thursday 12th

It's all systems go from today as your planet Mars enters Scorpio for the first time in two years. Focus on your personal goals and aims, get fit, get things moving and turn your attention to your image and profile. You might be in the news or take centre stage.

Friday 13th

Make a bold move and speak your mind. You may sense that things are starting to move in the right direction after a period of confusion or mixed emotions. Tap into the spooky reputation of Friday 13th and prove that you're not scared of diving into the dark places.

Saturday 14th

Today's solar eclipse is a strong symbol for letting something go. This might be giving up a habit, creating a clean slate or sweeping out dead wood to make space for new energy to come in. If you're planning a retreat, you're in tune with your stars.

Sunday 15th

You may discover a secret, something private or confidential that's been hidden from you. It's a good time to broach a difficult or sensitive subject and to do so with confidence. Be decisive in your actions and firm in your resolve. Other people will look to you to take charge.

Monday 16th

You might be in a position where you're hiring and firing over the next couple of days. At the very least, you're making decisions that impact other people's lives. It's rarely easy to be the one holding the front line, but you have the power and the strength to do so.

Tuesday 17th

If someone's not welcome in your home, be direct in your actions. Rather than beat around the bush, talk to them face to face and let them know what you see. You might be taking on a responsible role to protect a child or lover. Make the right move for everyone.

Wednesday 18th

It's not the best time to compare yourself to other people. Self-value and self-worth come from within. Do your inner work and learn to love yourself. You may be on the verge of a new chapter of personal transformation or growth. Support the process in any way you see fit.

Thursday 19th

It's easy to look outside of yourself for confirmation of who you are. If you're aware you're busy chasing fame or fortune without questioning it, do yourself a favour and stop to ask why. Once you recognise that you're enough exactly as you are, ambition becomes a choice.

Friday 20th

Use whatever tools are at your disposal to deepen the process of understanding, whether you journal, go to therapy or choose soul-work or healing. This is a time when you can learn to respond rather than react to life's challenges. It may start with taking a step back.

Saturday 21st

Look closely at your motivations and take care that you don't slip into power games. There's a shadow side to every star sign and yours is around how you wield your power. Use your energy to step into your power rather than spiral into self-destructive behaviour.

Sunday 22nd

Communication planet Mercury enters your star sign Scorpio today. This combination is great for psycho-analysis, psychic studies, research or detective work. If a serious conversation is on the cards, it's a great day to make it happen.

Monday 23rd

The Sun's move into Scorpio today gives you reason to celebrate. You often feel a shift in energy and an increase in confidence when the Sun enters your star sign. Put the past behind you and look to the future. Put your interests first and focus on your personal goals and aims.

Tuesday 24th

If you've been busy behind the scenes recently or hiding away, your opportunity to get noticed has arrived. You may have been building towards a new goal, studying, doing research or taking care of yourself. Either way, step into your power and let your light shine brightly.

Wednesday 25th

When it comes to love, it has to be a two-way connection. Rather than wish that a romantic relationship would come into being, be proactive and find out how someone feels about you. At the very least, you'll know where you stand and can channel your affections elsewhere.

Thursday 26th

Shut the door firmly on your dream world and engage head-on with life. When you doubt yourself or feel confused, make your first port of call physical activity. Get fit, go for a walk, go to the gym. Whatever gets your endorphins pumping around your body, do more of it.

Friday 27th

Keep busy today and get on top of your work and routine. There's some big astrology coming up over the next couple of days and you won't have time to deal with everyday matters. If you have a clear run to tick off your to-do list, leap to it. Being productive can be so satisfying.

Saturday 28th

Today's lunar eclipse is powerful for you. It's about getting relationships right. Sometimes, events come out of the blue during eclipse season that trigger change – one person wins while another person loses. The trick is to act fast and take advantage so you end up on the winning team.

Sunday 29th

If you're in a relationship that's not working out, expect hidden issues to emerge now. This is potentially a competitive or argumentative time. You might be in a triangle situation where you're vying against other people, whether this is regarding your love life or a business venture.

Monday 30th

If you're a typical Scorpio, you don't like to lose and you're not fond of change. If recent events have rocked you, regain your equilibrium. Take back your power and start by speaking your truth. That doesn't mean blaming someone else but being honest about your emotions.

Tuesday 31st

It often takes a while after an eclipse date for things to settle. If your actions have impacted other people, allow them time to talk and express their feelings. These are passionate stars and you may have no choice but to go all out to get what you want.

NOVEMBER
. . . .

Wednesday 1st

You may have some deep insight into what's happening in a friend's life. Yet, this isn't necessarily the time to step in and try to help. Sometimes, it's best to let things be and allow other people to create their own path of destiny. Be a diligent student this evening.

Thursday 2nd

Start looking ahead to 2024 and dream up some new plans and ideas. Forget your current limitations and allow your imagination full rein in coming up with a new wish list. Be optimistic and have faith that things will work out the way you want them to.

Friday 3rd

When it comes to a loving relationship, offer up your prayers but ultimately let go of things that have played out a certain way. It takes two to tango and, as much as you may want someone to love you, they may have their own agenda. A larger-than-life individual could help you get back on track.

Saturday 4th

Look closely at your motivations this weekend and take care you don't slip into power games. It might be time to step away from an online relationship that's not working out. In affairs of the heart and your personal life, come to terms with what's happening if you're ready to move on.

Sunday 5th

You may be at cross purposes with someone close. If you are starting to realise that the two of you have different hopes and dreams, it may be wise to consider your next steps and line up some new goals. Sometimes, you have to wait at a crossroads until inspiration strikes.

Monday 6th

As a Scorpio, you often have a keen understanding of other people's behaviour. Your laser focus and perceptive abilities help you read other people well. Trust your instincts today and initiate a conversation with one of your best friends.
Your support and insight could be invaluable to them.

Tuesday 7th

Dive deep into your emotions and seek fresh inspiration.
Do what feels right for you and take a step back from everyday life for a while. You may experience a sense of yearning or desire for a new romance. Help someone close to you make sense of a puzzle or question in their life.

Wednesday 8th

Follow your instincts and do what feels right today. It's important not to let other people control you or tell you what you can and can't do. If you want to venture into unknown territory regarding a romantic relationship, it's up to you.
A secret liaison could be the passion you're seeking.

Thursday 9th

You may be involved in giving a talk or presentation today. You might be writing a blog or getting your voice heard. The good news is that people will listen to what you have to say, so share your wisdom and experience. Be supportive of younger people.

Friday 10th

This is an ideal time to meditate and create some space and quiet to sit and listen. It's especially important if you have a big decision to make around money. Do whatever's right so you can stop worrying and feel more safe and secure. Take a deep breath and move on.

Saturday 11th

Try not to get involved in an argument today, even if you feel angry when someone lets you down. Put yourself first and look after your needs. Acting impulsively isn't wise, especially if you're accident-prone. Don't hold on to bad feelings now. Ditch the past and look to the future.

Sunday 12th

You're on the verge of a new moon in your star sign. This is the ideal time to consider how far you've come in the past year and what you want for yourself moving forwards. Set your intentions and make some bold resolutions that point your compass in a new direction.

Monday 13th

You can't ignore the new moon in Scorpio that takes place today. Look to your personal goals, your image and profile, your desires and passion. You may choose to break free and do what's required to take back your power. This new moon could flag up a fresh start in a relationship.

Tuesday 14th

Get back on board with your money goals as it's an excellent day to talk finances. You may be able to clear up a financial issue that's linked to an ex or someone from your past. If you want to treat someone close, you could come across a gift that's perfect for them.

Wednesday 15th

Bring some clarity and sensitivity to your relationships today. A lunchtime meeting or get-together would be perfect if you want to talk about money. If a child or a lover in your life is living in a fantasy world, help them view their situation with clarity, especially around love or money.

Thursday 16th

Keep the lines of communication open and don't let someone close off the hook if they haven't yet committed to a plan of action. If you're typical of your star sign, you know how to stay on track with your goals. This is your opportunity to give sound advice to someone you care about.

Friday 17th

It could be a stunning weekend for romance as passions rise. Don't hold back if you've lined up a date or you're keen to get to know someone close on a deeper level. Scorpio's element is water, which means you tend to respond emotionally. Engage whole-heartedly with life.

Saturday 18th

Put your mind to it and you could achieve anything today.
The stars are aligned for you to turn your laser focus towards a
personal goal or a community or neighbourhood venture that
matters to you deeply. Your ambition is backed up by a strong
will to get things done.

Sunday 19th

Spend some time at home today in the bosom of your family.
If there's a relative you haven't seen for a while, it would be
a good day to visit or reconnect over the airwaves. If you're
in a relationship or married, make a point of doing things
separately and reclaim your independence.

Monday 20th

Secrets may be uncovered now and there could be more than
one puzzle or mystery to unravel. This is potentially a week
of revelation. You may be ready to step into your power, speak
with conviction and mean what you say. Show your support for
a neighbourhood scheme.

Tuesday 21st

This is a go-for-it period when you're being called forth to
make a difference. Be determined and fearless. Yet, at the
same time, be aware that your strong personality can prove
overpowering for some people. Reconsider how important it is
that you get your way today.

Wednesday 22nd

Money matters fall under the cosmic spotlight as the Sun enters your money zone. Other people could step in to help you financially. Or, you find a new money-making outlet through your work or an online venture. Explore all your options around money and finances.

Thursday 23rd

The Sun's move into your money zone is a time to trust your luck. There could be some good fortune on the way. However, before it arrives on your doorstep, you may have to cut costs or put up with a cash disappointment. Close the door on a financial project that's not working out.

Friday 24th

Money matters get a surge of energy as your ruling planet, Mars, joins the Sun in your money zone. You might be out shopping or be keen to make more money today. Turn your ambitious nature towards this important area of your life, increase your prices and make some smart money moves.

Saturday 25th

Recognise what you can and can't achieve now. Some things are worth fighting for, and sometimes, you have to learn to let go. Don't wear yourself out trying to achieve the impossible, especially if a child or lover is in trouble again.

Sunday 26th

Notice when you're feeling angry. Anger's not a bad emotion as long as it's channelled effectively. Ensure you use your anger to good effect to help someone close change their habits for the better. Be resolute and determined in your actions. Do what you say.

Monday 27th

Don't ignore money matters this week as the light of the full moon could reveal more. You may need to get tough where other people are concerned, especially if you're helping someone out financially. Confront a personal issue head-on and don't allow a situation to drag interminably.

Tuesday 28th

Sometimes, the best way to help someone is to let go. That's what you might consider now under the rays of the full moon. Be kind and caring but don't collude with someone close. Also, make sure you're paid what you're worth and chase up any outstanding payments.

Wednesday 29th

Seek new people and new inspiration in your life. If you're dealing with the same old issues, it's important to have some plans and ideas to look forward to. Fire some arrows high into the sky to see where they land in 2024. Research a holiday or workshop that you'd like to attend.

Thursday 30th

Breathe some new life into an old problem and look at an issue from an upside-down angle. This is a great time for lateral thinking. Get your best mate to help you, the one who knows how to view life differently. Be spontaneous in your relationships and affairs of the heart.

DECEMBER

. . . .

Friday 1st

You may have a deep conversation with someone today. Or, perhaps your words have power and you experience a soulmate connection. Get more involved in your local community or neighbourhood and find out what's happening close to home over the festive period.

Saturday 2nd

Keep your eye on the ball when it comes to work and money and don't let your ambitious nature slide. That being said, it's an excellent day for catching up with your relatives, a sibling or neighbour. Have a grown-up conversation with a child and broach a serious matter.

Sunday 3rd

A romantic relationship could turn complex because of the intensity of your emotions. If you're drawn to someone and the feeling isn't mutual, consider letting go and move on. It's only when you fully close a door on the past that you allow new energy and people to step in.

Monday 4th

The planet of love, Venus, moves into Scorpio today. When Venus is in your star sign, you often attract good things into your life. Pay more attention to your image and profile, whether you get your hair done or buy some new clothes for the upcoming festive parties.

Tuesday 5th

If you're looking for love, this is a gorgeous time to go all out to find it and say yes to romance. You have the goddess of love, Venus, blessing your star sign, so make the most of it. In your close relationships, speak from the heart and let other people know you care.

Wednesday 6th

This would be a lovely day to fall deep into your emotions and experience your feelings fully. It's not the best day to go out drinking, if you know you have to be on top form at work over the next two days. If you're seeking something more to life, choose your activities wisely.

Thursday 7th

Other people may leave money up to you on the run-up to the festive period. They might appreciate your knowledge and your ability to get the best bargains or keep tabs on who's spending what. You have an eye for equality and your dealings will be fair.

Friday 8th

You have the gift of the gab and you can use it to your advantage today. You might be taking the lead fundraising or organising a charity event. If so, trust your intuition in knowing who's the best person for which job. A chance conversation could quickly lead to something more.

Saturday 9th

This is potentially an exciting weekend for your love life as you have big planet Jupiter bringing a new opportunity your way. You might like what it brings you immensely. A relationship could reach new heights so long as you throw yourself in with gusto and enthusiasm.

Sunday 10th

A relationship doesn't have to be conventional for it to be right. With Uranus racking up the alternative vibes in your relationship zone, it's best to remain open-minded as anything goes. Someone who's not your usual type could prove to be the perfect partner for you.

Monday 11th

You'll know a relationship's on the right track when you can't stop texting or talking to one another. If you're a typical Scorpio, you give yourself wholeheartedly to love as you have a huge capacity for passion and depth of feeling. Draw the right kind of people into your life.

Tuesday 12th

Today's new moon takes place in your money zone. If you want to earn more money before the end of the year, check out a new earning opportunity today. If you want to draw up a budget or make a list of presents and expenses, this is a perfect time to do so.

Wednesday 13th

It's a high energy new moon and a good time to focus on your future and where you're heading. What do you want to invest in? What do you value highly in life? Money and self-worth are closely connected. This is where positive change is highlighted over the next few weeks.

Thursday 14th

Communication planet Mercury is retrograde, but this isn't necessarily a bad thing. Admittedly, you may find that getting from A to B takes longer than usual and it's important to double-check all your communications. However, if it brings someone back into your life, it gets the thumbs-up.

Friday 15th

You may be busier than usual today. Perhaps you're trying to get things wrapped up so you can have a long break over the festive period. Your levels of concentration could be impressive, and if so, use them wisely. This evening, put your feet up at home, chill out and relax.

Saturday 16th

The moon is in your home and family zone all weekend. If you're putting up the decorations or visiting relatives, you're in tune with your stars. If you're a typical Scorpio, you like to be organised and you're not usually a last-minute merchant. Sort things out at home.

Sunday 17th

Keep close tabs on your money today and don't let cash slip through your fingers. You could easily be overly indulgent. Or, you might get careless around cash and possessions. The charitable side of your nature will be called forth, but only give what you can afford.

Monday 18th

If someone has put a smile on your face, don't wait for them to contact you. This is a lovely day to reach out to people and connect with others. It would be a good time to chase information, find out a test result or meet your neighbours.

Tuesday 19th

You're likely to be in a festive mood today. You might not be able to take your eye off work completely but don't let that stop you from making the most of this social time of year. The emphasis is on play and good times. Say yes to a last-minute social event.

Wednesday 20th

Someone could let you down at work, which means you have to do more than your fair share. If you put your mind to it and concentrate on the job at hand, you could race through your to-do list at record speed. Don't spend time complaining when you could be working.

Thursday 21st

Your stars feel excitable. It's a good day for a heart-to-heart, especially if someone close has been behaving out of character and you want to know the reason why. Mercury remains retrograde, so you may need to chop and change your schedule to accommodate other people.

Friday 22nd

You'll be delighted if someone reaches out to you and makes amends for a previous misdemeanour. Love is in the ascendancy at lunchtime and again after work. A person's generosity could make your day. You'll be dining out on the experience for weeks.

Saturday 23rd

Communication planet Mercury dips back into your money zone today. You may be reconsidering your gifts or expenses. If you're doing everything on your own, including paying out, take swift action so this doesn't continue. It's important to get a partner or co-worker on your side.

Sunday 24th

Park any gripes that you may have about money and resolve to come back to them after the festive break. This isn't the time to be a grinch, so put a smile on your face and join in with the festivities. This evening, be social and enjoy yourself at a local pub or with your family.

Monday 25th

This could be an extra special day. Perhaps you've decided to forego the family festivities to be with a new lover or indulge your romantic side. As long as your passionate nature is engaged, it could truly be a wonderful day.

Tuesday 26th

Even though you may have resolved not to talk about money over the festive period, your best intentions could go by the wayside today. Bring up the topic and it's bound to be argumentative. Do yourself a favour and take yourself off to the local pantomime.

Wednesday 27th

Today's full moon highlights your travel zone. This would be the perfect date to plan a trip for next year if you're not abroad already. Catch up with family who live abroad or in a different part of the country. Reach out and make connections and strangers could become friends.

Thursday 28th

Avoid the sales, as it would be easy for you to overspend at the shops and get carried away. Your willpower could go out of the window when you're lured by a bargain. In a similar vein, don't get carried away romantically as this could leave you feeling confused.

Friday 29th

Love and travel are linked, so plan a holiday with your other half or go away over the New Year weekend. It's a better date for relationships, as you're less likely to cling and become overly emotional. A foreigner or independent traveller could win your heart.

Saturday 30th

If you're working today, you won't be happy about it but your partner's the one who could be truly miffed. You're more likely to soldier on and do what's necessary. A love relationship or business partnership could take a turn for the better on New Year's Eve – it's celebration time.

Sunday 31st

Today's stars are positively lovely for love, luck and good fortune. Look out for a gift or bonus that comes your way. There might be a reason to celebrate your partner's good fortune. Or, perhaps you benefit when Lady Luck favours someone close to you. Enjoy a night out with your friends.

Scorpio

·················

PEOPLE WHO
YOUR SIGN

PEOPLE WHO SHARE YOUR SIGN

· · · · · · · · · · · · · · · · · ·

Scorpios have seduced our screens for decades, from Goldie Hawn to Scarlett Johansson, so it's no wonder that they have a reputation for being the sexiest sign in the zodiac calendar. The Scorpion is a mysterious creature that has brought dark depths to the world in the form of Martin Scorsese's films, and wonders of entertainment in the form of RuPaul's Drag Race. Discover which of these intriguing Scorpios share your exact birthday and see if you can spot the similarities.

24th October
Shenae Grimes (1989), Eliza Taylor (1989), Drake (1986), Wayne Rooney (1985), Katie McGrath (1983), Roman Abramovich (1966), Malcolm Turnbull, Australian Prime Minister (1954), Kevin Kline (1947)

25th October
Rylan Clark-Neal (1988), Ciara (1985), Katy Perry (1984), Craig Robinson (1971), David Furnish (1962), Chad Smith (1961), Pablo Picasso (1881), Johann Strauss II (1825)

26th October
Seth MacFarlane (1973), Phaedra Parks (1973), Tom Cavanagh (1968), Keith Urban (1967), Uhuru Kenyatta, Kenyan President (1961), Dylan McDermott (1961), Rita Wilson (1956), Hillary Clinton (1947), Jaclyn Smith (1945)

27th October

Kelly Osbourne (1984), Marla Maples (1963), Simon Le Bon (1958), Luiz Inácio Lula da Silva, Brazilian President (1945), John Cleese (1939), Sylvia Plath (1932), Roy Lichtenstein (1923), Theodore Roosevelt, U.S. President (1858)

28th October

Frank Ocean (1987), Troian Bellisario (1985), Matt Smith (1982), Joaquin Phoenix (1974), Julia Roberts (1967), Matt Drudge (1966), Bill Gates (1955), Caitlyn Jenner (1949)

29th October

Tove Lo (1987), Ben Foster (1980), Tracee Ellis Ross (1972), Gabrielle Union (1972), Winona Ryder (1971), Rufus Sewell (1967), Kate Jackson (1948), Richard Dreyfuss (1947)

30th October

Janel Parrish (1988), Clémence Poésy (1982), Ivanka Trump (1981), Matthew Morrison (1978), Nia Long (1970), Gavin Rossdale (1965), Diego Maradona (1960), Timothy B. Schmit (1947), Henry Winkler (1945)

31st October

Willow Smith (2000), Frank Iero (1981), Piper Perabo (1976),Vanilla Ice (1967), Rob Schneider (1963), Peter Jackson (1961), John Candy (1950), Zaha Hadid (1950), Michael Landon (1936), Carlos Drummond de Andrade (1902), Sardar Patel (1875)

1st November

Penn Badgley (1986), Aishwarya Rai (1973), Jenny McCarthy (1972), Jeremy Hunt (1966), Anthony Kiedis (1962), Tim Cook (1960), David Foster (1949), Larry Flynt (1942)

2nd November

Nelly (1974), Stevie J (1971), David Schwimmer (1966), Shahrukh Khan (1965), Warren G. Harding, U.S. President (1865), James Knox Polk, U.S. President (1795), Marie Antionette (1755)

3rd November

Kendall Jenner (1995), Colin Kaepernick (1987), Gabe Newell (1962), Dolph Lundgren (1957), Kate Capshaw (1953), Larry Holmes (1949), Anna Wintour (1949)

4th November

Jessa Seewald (1992), Dez Bryant (1988), Guy Martin (1981), Bethenny Frankel (1970), P. Diddy (1969), Matthew McConaughey (1969), Ralph Macchio (1961), Kathy Griffin (1960)

5th November

Virat Kohli (1988), Kevin Jonas (1987), Alexa Chung (1983), Luke Hemsworth (1981), Danniella Westbrook (1973), Famke Janssen (1964), Tilda Swinton (1960), Bryan Adams (1959), Kris Jenner (1955)

6th November

Kris Wu (1990), Emma Stone (1988), Conchita Wurst (1988), Taryn Manning (1978), Thandie Newton (1972), Rebecca Romijn (1972), Ethan Hawke (1970), Kelly Rutherford (1968), Mohamed Hadid (1948), Sally Field (1946)

7th November

Lorde (1996), Bethany Mota (1995), David de Gea (1990), Elsa Hosk (1988), David Guetta (1967), Joni Mitchell (1943), Albert Camus (1913), Marie Curie (1867)

8th November

Jasmine Thompson (2000), Lauren Alaina (1994), Jessica Lowndes (1988), Erica Mena (1987) Tara Reid (1975), Tech N9ne (1971), Gordon Ramsay (1966), Bonnie Raitt (1949), Alain Delon (1935)

9th November

French Montana (1984), Caroline Flack (1979), Nick Lachey (1973), Eric Dane (1972), Lou Ferrigno (1951), Carl Sagan (1934), Hedy Lamarr (1914), Muhammad Iqbal (1877)

10th November

Mackenzie Foy (2000), Kiernan Shipka (1999), Zoey Deutch (1994), Taron Egerton (1989), Josh Peck (1986), Miranda Lambert (1983), Diplo (1978), Eve (1978), Brittany Murphy (1977), Ellen Pompeo (1969), Hugh Bonneville (1963), Neil Gaiman (1960)

11th November

Tye Sheridan (1996), Vinny Guadagnino (1987), Philipp Lahm (1983), Leonardo DiCaprio (1974), Calista Flockhart (1964), Demi Moore (1962), Stanley Tucci (1960), Kurt Vonnegut (1922), Fyodor Dostoevsky (1821)

12th November

Anne Hathaway (1982), Ryan Gosling (1980), Gustaf Skarsgård (1980), Tonya Harding (1970), Nadia Comăneci (1961), Megan Mullally (1958), Hassan Rouhani, Iranian President (1948), Neil Young (1945), Grace Kelly (1929)

13th November

Matt Bennett (1991), Devon Bostick (1991), Gerard Butler (1969), Jimmy Kimmel (1967), Steve Zahn (1967), Whoopi Goldberg (1955), Chris Noth (1954), Frances Conroy (1953), Andrés Manuel López Obrador, Mexican President-elect (1953), Robert Louis Stevenson (1850)

14th November

Russell Tovey (1981), Olga Kurylenko (1979), Travis Barker (1975), Gary Vaynerchuk (1975), Josh Duhamel (1972), Patrick Warburton (1964), Charles, Prince of Wales (1948), Astrid Lindgren (1907), Claude Monet (1840)

15th November

Paulo Dybala (1993), Shailene Woodley (1991), B.o.B (1988), Sania Mirza (1986), Lily Aldridge (1985), Jeffree Star (1985), Chad Kroeger (1974), Jonny Lee Miller (1972), Jimmy Choo (1948)

16th November

Pete Davidson (1993), Vicky Pattison (1987), Gemma Atkinson (1984), Maggie Gyllenhaal (1977), Paul Scholes (1974), Brandi Glanville (1972), Missi Pyle (1972), Lisa Bonet (1967), Sheree Zampino (1967)

17th November

Tom Ellis (1978), Rachel McAdams (1978), Lorraine Pascale (1972), Jeff Buckley (1966), Jonathan Ross (1960), RuPaul (1960), Danny DeVito (1944), Lauren Hutton (1943), Martin Scorsese (1942)

18th November

Nick Bateman (1986), Fabolous (1977), Anthony McPartlin (1975), Chloë Sevigny (1974), Owen Wilson (1968), Kirk Hammett (1962), Elizabeth Perkins (1960), Kim Wilde (1960), Linda Evans (1942)

19th November

Tyga (1989), Adam Driver (1983), Jack Dorsey (1976), Jodie Foster (1962), Meg Ryan (1961), Allison Janney (1959), Charlie Kaufman (1958), Calvin Klein (1942), Larry King (1933), Indira Gandhi, Indian Prime Minister (1917)

20th November

Michael Clifford (1995), Oliver Sykes (1986), Future (1983), Andrea Riseborough (1981), Kimberley Walsh (1981), Ming-Na Wen (1963), Sean Young (1959), Bo Derek (1956), Joe Walsh (1947)

21st November

Conor Maynard (1992), Colleen Ballinger (1986), Carly Rae Jepsen (1985), Jena Malone (1984), Nikki Bella (1983), Ken Block (1967), Björk (1965), Nicollette Sheridan (1963), Goldie Hawn (1945), René Magritte (1898)

22nd November

Hailey Baldwin (1996), Alden Ehrenreich (1989), Scarlett Johansson (1984), Boris Becker (1967), Mark Ruffalo (1967), Mads Mikkelsen (1965), Jamie Lee Curtis (1958), Rodney Dangerfield (1921)